RECLAIM JOY

Self-help Strategies for Positive Mental health

By
Carol Moore

Text Copyright 2024 – © Carol Moore.
All rights reserved worldwide. No part of this publication may be republished in any form or by any means, including photocopying, scanning, or otherwise, without prior written permission from the author.

Table of Content

INTRODUCTION 9

CHAPTER 1: THE BASICS OF MENTAL HEALTH 13

CHAPTER 2: IDENTIFYING YOUR STRUGGLES 16

Common Symptoms and Signs 18

Root Causes 19

End of Chapter Reflection 21

CHAPTER 3: THE STIGMA OF MENTAL HEALTH 24

Personal and Societal Impact 25

Overcoming Stigma 27

End of Chapter Reflection 29

CHAPTER 4: CONQUERING ANXIETY 33

Mindfulness Techniques 34

Cognitive-Behavioral Strategies 35

Lifestyle Modifications 37

End of Chapter Reflection 38

CHAPTER 5: OVERCOMING DEPRESSION 41

Causes of Depression 41

Symptoms of Depression 43

Types of Depression 45

Creating Routines 47

Finding Joy in Small Things 49

Positive Affirmations 49

End of Chapter Reflection 50

CHAPTER 6: BUILDING SELF-CONFIDENCE AND SELF-ESTEEM 53

Daily Confidence Boosters 54

Challenging Negative Thoughts 55

Self-Compassion Exercises 56

End of Chapter Reflection 58

CHAPTER 7: HEALING FROM TRAUMA 61

Types of Trauma 61

Grounding Techniques 63

The Power of Storytelling 65

Seeking Professional Help 67

End of Chapter Reflection 70

CHAPTER 8: IMPROVING BODY IMAGE 73

Self-Acceptance Practices 75

Media Literacy 78

Body-Positive Lifestyle Changes 80

End of Chapter Reflection 82

CHAPTER 9: CREATING A PERSONAL MENTAL HEALTH PLAN 87

Setting Clear Goals 87

Developing a Routine 90

Adjusting Your Plan 92

End of Chapter Reflection 95

CHAPTER 10: BUILDING A SUPPORT SYSTEM 97

Identifying Supportive People 98

Joining Support Groups 100

End of Chapter Reflection 102

CHAPTER 11: THE POWER OF MINDFULNESS AND MEDITATION 105

Daily Mindfulness Practices 106

Beginner Meditation Techniques 106

Advanced Mindfulness Strategies 107

End of Chapter Reflection 108

CHAPTER 12: MAINTAINING MENTAL HEALTH IN CHALLENGING TIMES 112

Resilience Building 112

Coping with Setbacks 113

Developing a Positive Mindset 114

Lifelong Learning for Mental Health 114

Setting New Goals 115

End of Chapter Reflection 116

CONCLUSION 118

Author's Note

Over the years, I've had the privilege of listening to the stories of people from all walks of life. No matter their background, career, or success, one thing unites them: the struggle to overcome the pain and challenges brought on by mental health battles. I've seen some of the most accomplished individuals wrestle with anxiety and self-doubt. The kindest people, who would never judge others harshly, often turn that judgment inward on themselves. And many of those who appear joyful and confident to the outside world are often left feeling overwhelmed and lost when they are alone. Does that sound familiar? Perhaps you've experienced these feelings too.

Mental health affects every aspect of your life—the way you connect with others, the decisions you make, and the joy you feel each day. Have you ever wondered why it's so hard to feel truly at peace, even when everything seems fine on the outside? I've come to realize that while our external lives may seem full, true peace and happiness are often missing for so many. My passion for mental health comes from witnessing these struggles firsthand and wanting to be a voice of hope, compassion, and practical guidance for those who feel weighed down by their thoughts and emotions.

You may ask why, in a time when we have access to so much materially, so many people are still unhappy? Why are we consumed with worry, self-criticism, and constant comparisons to others? These are questions I've asked myself countless times, and they have fueled my desire to write this book. I noticed a gap in the resources available for mental health—a lack of practical advice delivered with deep empathy. I wanted to create something that feels like a comforting guide for you, something you can turn to in moments of doubt, knowing you aren't alone and that there's a path forward to reclaiming your joy. My hope is that as you read this book, you'll find strategies that speak to your heart and mind. Whether you're struggling with anxiety, self-doubt, or the pressures of daily life, I want this book to help you rediscover joy, feel supported, and understand that you have the power to transform your mental well-being.

And to you, the reader, thank you for choosing this book and trusting me to be part of your journey toward better mental health. I hope these words serve as a source of encouragement, inspiration, and practical support as you reclaim your joy.

I'd love to hear from you! If you have thoughts, experiences, or feedback after reading this book, kindly reach out to me. You can connect with me through the following channel:
http://moorepositivepsychology.com. Your journey is unique, and your input is invaluable—not just to me, but to others on the path of reclaiming their joy.

Introduction

"Joy does not simply happen to us. We have to choose joy and keep choosing it every day." — Henri Nouwen.

Do you ever feel like joy has slipped through your fingers, lost somewhere amidst the weight of your daily struggles? You're not alone if it feels like joy is a distant memory that's slowly faded over time. Maybe you remember a period when happiness came easily, when waking up each morning felt light, full of possibility. But somewhere along the way, life's pressures, worries, and that constant buzz of anxiety have taken over. Can you relate to this? Have you found yourself wondering why joy is so hard to hold onto, why it seems like others have it figured out while you're left feeling stuck?

Take a moment—right now—and think about how you've been feeling recently. Have the challenges in your life left you emotionally drained, mentally exhausted? How long has it been since you truly felt joy, not just fleeting moments of happiness, but that deep, lasting joy that brings peace and contentment? How has this weighed on your relationships, your work, or even how you see yourself? It's not uncommon to feel like this joy is out of reach, but let me assure you, it's not. Reclaiming your joy is within your reach. Together, we'll explore practical steps to help you regain control over your mental health and bring that joy back into your life.

Mental health issues such as anxiety, depression, and low self-esteem are more prevalent than many people realize. Maybe you've noticed it in your own life or heard from others who are struggling. Did you know that anxiety disorders affect more than **284 million p**eople worldwide, making it the most common mental health condition? Depression, equally widespread, impacts over **264 million** people globally. With these staggering numbers, it's clear that many of us are dealing with the same emotional and psychological challenges. You're not alone in this. But the question remains—why is it so difficult to maintain joy, especially when faced with these mental health challenges?

Think about the factors that may have played a role in making joy seem so far away. The constant societal pressure to be more, do more, and achieve more can be overwhelming. Add to that unresolved trauma or the relentless pace of modern life, and it's no wonder that joy feels elusive. Have you found yourself comparing your life to others, feeling like you're falling short? Or perhaps past experiences have left emotional scars that still influence how you view yourself today. These feelings, over time, can take a toll on not just your mental and emotional health, but on every aspect of your life—your relationships, your career, your sense of purpose. Can you see how this disconnection from joy has affected you personally?

But here's the good news—joy isn't something that's permanently lost. It's not a thing of the past and certainly isn't reserved for others. Joy can be reclaimed, step by step, through deliberate, mindful actions. This book is here to help you navigate that journey. It's not just a collection of advice—it's a guide, a supportive companion designed to walk with you as you work through the emotional and mental challenges you face. Does that sound like something you're ready for? Because I'm ready to help you get there.

Why this book? What makes it different? Well, for one, it's written with you in mind. Every page is designed to offer both empathy and practical strategies, tailored specifically to the mental health challenges many of us face today. You'll find tools for overcoming anxiety, healing from trauma, building your self-esteem, and improving how you see yourself—inside and out. And these aren't just surface-level fixes; they're strategies that, when practiced consistently, will support your mental well-being for the long term. Does that sound like the kind of transformation you're looking for?

Beyond just offering advice, this book will empower you to take control of your mental health journey. You might seek help from professionals, and that's incredibly valuable, but there's something deeply empowering about using self-help strategies to guide your own recovery. In these pages, you'll find interactive exercises, journaling prompts, and practical activities designed to engage you actively. You won't just read—you'll participate. These elements are meant to be tools you use, day in and day out, to create real change.

Now, I know you may be wondering how to navigate through all this. Here's the thing—you can read this book from start to finish or jump to the sections that speak to you the most right now. The structure is flexible, allowing you to go at your own pace and revisit what resonates with you whenever you need it. Each time you engage with the material, it will meet you where you are, whether you're just beginning your journey or already well along the path to reclaiming your joy.

So, as you move forward, I encourage you to approach this book with an open heart and an open mind. Remember, the journey to reclaiming joy is deeply personal and won't always be easy. But with patience, effort, and a good dose of self-compassion, you'll get there. Joy is not something that happens to you—it's something you choose. And with the steps laid out in this book, you'll learn how to keep choosing joy, every single day.

Happy reading—and welcome to the first step in reclaiming the joy that is yours.

PART ONE:
UNDERSTANDING MENTAL HEALTH

Chapter 1: The Basics of Mental Health

"Mental health is not a destination, but a process. It's about how you drive, not where you're going." — Noam Shpancer.

What comes to mind when you hear the words *mental health*? Do you think of peace, or perhaps the difficult times, the struggles you've faced along the way? It's easy to assume mental health is something either "good" or "bad"—a switch that's either on or off. But the truth is, mental health is much more than just one state of being. It's constantly shifting, shaped by your emotions, thoughts, and interactions with the world around you. Have you ever stopped to think about how your mental health affects your day-to-day life?

Let's take a moment to really consider that. Mental health isn't just about feeling happy or content. It's about how you manage stress, how you handle challenges, how you relate to the people in y go our life, and even how you feel about yourself. It touches every part of who you are—emotionally, psychologically, and socially. You might ask yourself: When life throws unexpected difficulties my way, how do I respond? How does it affect my relationships, my work, or my sense of self-worth? The way you handle these moments speaks volumes about your mental health, whether you've realized it before or not.

Think of your mental health as existing on a sliding scale. Some days, you might feel mentally strong, balanced, and capable—like you've got everything under control. But then, there are times when stress, anxiety, or doubt seem to take over, making even the simplest tasks feel overwhelming. This back-and-forth shift is completely normal. Life throws different challenges our way, and it's only natural that your mental health fluctuates in response. Have you noticed these shifts in your own life? Maybe you were feeling steady and strong last week, and today, things feel more difficult. That's okay. What matters most is recognizing where you are on this scale.

Just like your physical health, your mental health changes over time. It's not static—it ebbs and flows. Some days feel easier, while others may challenge you more. This is why it's so important to regularly check in with yourself. Are you aware of the patterns? Do certain situations or stressors trigger stronger reactions, nudging you toward anxiety or stress? By paying attention to these changes, you can start to understand how to navigate the ups and downs with greater awareness.

And when we talk about mental health, we can't ignore the big challenges that many of us face at some point in our lives. Anxiety—does that word resonate with you? Maybe you've experienced the kind of persistent worry that hangs over your day like a cloud. Or perhaps depression has been something you've dealt with, a feeling of heaviness that makes even the simplest tasks feel overwhelming. Then, there's trauma—those past events that don't seem to let go, following you into the present, shaping your thoughts and emotions long after they've occurred. These challenges are very real and very common. And yes, we'll explore them in much more detail as we go deeper into this book. But for now, can you relate to any of these experiences? Have you ever found yourself battling these struggles, even when you don't fully understand where they came from?

It's easy to think that because you're dealing with these struggles, something is "wrong" with you. But the reality is, mental health challenges are just part of the human experience. They don't define you, and they don't have to control you. What's important is recognizing how these issues show up in your life. Have you taken the time to consider how anxiety or depression might be affecting you—not just emotionally, but in your relationships, your work, or your day-to-day routine? How has the way you see yourself changed because of it?

Understanding your mental health starts with identifying the struggles you face. Have you ever noticed patterns in your thoughts or behaviors that you can't seem to break? Do you find yourself reacting the same way to certain situations, even when you try to do things differently? These are the kinds of questions that start to unlock a deeper understanding of yourself, and the answers might surprise you. Recognizing these patterns is the first step toward changing them.

But before we dive into the details of anxiety, depression, or other challenges, let's think about what your specific struggles might be. Have you ever stopped to ask yourself why you respond the way you do? What are the obstacles standing in your way? These are the questions we'll be exploring next. And when we do, you'll start to see that understanding your struggles is key to overcoming them.

Chapter 2: Identifying Your Struggles

"The more you know yourself, the more clarity there is. Self-knowledge has no end." — *Jiddu Krishnamurti.*

How well do you know yourself? Not just the surface-level stuff—like your favorite hobbies or foods—but really, deeply understand what makes you feel anxious or why certain situations trigger doubt or sadness? So often, we go through life experiencing emotions without stopping to ask ourselves why. Why do you react the way you do? What are the underlying feelings driving your reactions? The key to making sense of your mental health journey begins with recognizing and identifying your personal struggles. Only then can you start to find the right path to healing.

One way to begin is by using self-assessment tools. Have you ever taken the time to reflect on what mental health challenges are affecting you most? Maybe you've already felt the weight of anxiety, or perhaps there's a lingering sense of sadness that seems to color your days. But identifying these feelings is more than just knowing they exist—it's about pinpointing what exactly you're struggling with, so you can work through them step by step.

Self-assessment tools, like questionnaires and mood trackers, are designed to help you dive deeper into your emotional and mental state. Let's talk about questionnaires for a moment. These aren't your average "yes" or "no" questions; they're thoughtfully crafted to help you uncover the root of your emotions. Have you ever wondered why you feel anxious in certain situations but not in others? Or why some days you wake up feeling down for no apparent reason? A well-designed questionnaire can prompt you to think about how often you experience certain feelings, what triggers them, and how they affect your daily life. By simply answering these questions, you begin to piece together a more complete picture of what's happening beneath the surface. It's like turning the lights on in a dark room—suddenly, everything that seemed hidden becomes clearer.

Now, let's look at mood trackers. Have you ever found yourself feeling off for a few days but not knowing why? Mood trackers allow you to chart your emotions over time, helping you see patterns that might otherwise go unnoticed. It's easy to dismiss a bad mood as "just one of those days," but when you track your feelings daily, you start to see trends. Do certain times of the month, specific environments, or interactions with particular people consistently affect your mood? A mood tracker can be as simple as a journal where you jot down how you're feeling each day, or it can be more structured, using apps designed specifically for this purpose. The idea is to help you connect the dots between your emotions and your daily experiences.

Imagine this: You've been tracking your mood for a week and notice that whenever you have a difficult conversation at work, you feel anxious for the rest of the day. Or maybe you realize that your mood consistently drops after spending time with a certain friend. These aren't things you'd necessarily catch in the moment, but when you look back over a week or a month of tracking, patterns begin to emerge. Once you see those patterns, you can start making changes to manage or even avoid the triggers that contribute to your mental health struggles.

These tools are like a road map for your emotional health. They give you a starting point, a way to understand what's really going on inside. And once you have that understanding, you can begin making decisions that support your well-being. So, how often are you checking in with yourself? Have you ever tried mapping out your feelings and reactions in this way? You might be surprised by what you discover about yourself.

Common Symptoms and Signs

Let's break down some common mental health challenges—anxiety, depression, low self-esteem, and trauma. These issues often sneak into your life in different ways—sometimes subtly, sometimes with overwhelming force. Recognizing the signs early is crucial because it allows you to understand what's happening within and take the necessary steps toward healing.

- **Anxiety:** Do you often feel like your mind is running at a million miles per hour, jumping from one worry to the next? Anxiety can manifest in many ways, from constant, nagging worries about the future to physical symptoms like a racing heart or trouble sleeping. You might find yourself stuck in a loop of "what ifs," imagining worst-case scenarios, even when everything seems fine. Sound familiar? Anxiety tends to creep in, distorting your perception of reality and making even small tasks feel monumental.

- **Depression:** Unlike anxiety, depression often feels like a heavy fog that clouds your ability to experience joy or motivation. It's more than just sadness—it's an overwhelming sense of emptiness or hopelessness that can make even getting out of bed feel like an impossible task. Have you ever felt like the things that used to bring you happiness now seem meaningless? This is the grip of depression, pulling you away from the things that once mattered most.

- **Low Self-Esteem:** When you look in the mirror, what do you see? Low self-esteem is like carrying a constant critic in your mind, always reminding you of your flaws or shortcomings. It's the voice that tells you that you're not good enough, not smart enough, not deserving of success or happiness. Over time, these thoughts can become a filter through which you view yourself, casting a shadow over everything you do.

- **Trauma:** Trauma is a lingering force that stays with you long after the initial event has passed. Whether it's from a single traumatic experience or prolonged exposure to harmful situations, trauma can leave deep emotional scars that affect your mental health. You might find yourself triggered by certain sights, sounds, or experiences that remind you of the past, causing an emotional response that feels as fresh as the day it happened. Does that resonate with you?

Root Causes

Understanding these symptoms is only part of the puzzle. To truly address your struggles, you must look at their origins. Mental health challenges don't arise in isolation—they are often shaped by internal and external factors. It's like peeling back the layers of an onion. The symptoms you experience are just the outer layer, but beneath that are deeper influences that contribute to how you feel and why you react the way you do. So, have you ever wondered where your struggles really begin? Let's explore some of the most common root causes that could be affecting you.

First, think about **genetics.** You've probably heard people say things like, "It runs in the family," when it comes to certain health conditions. Well, mental health is no different. Have you ever stopped and thought about whether some of your emotions—like feeling anxious or low—might be linked to your family's history? Maybe you've noticed that a parent or sibling has struggled with anxiety or depression, too. Genetics can play a role, making you more likely to experience certain mental health challenges. It doesn't mean you're destined to feel this way forever, though. But doesn't it feel a little freeing to know that part of what you're going through might have roots that go back further than you realized? It's not all about what's happening right now—sometimes, it's about what's been passed down. Knowing this can help you understand that these feelings aren't your fault, but part of the bigger picture.

Now, let's shift to your **environment.** What was it like where you grew up? Were you surrounded by support and love, or was your home filled with stress, conflict, or even uncertainty? The environment you were raised in can shape the way you see the world now, how you deal with challenges, and even how you handle relationships. For example, if you grew up in a place where tension was always high, you might have learned to walk on eggshells or become hyper-aware of other people's emotions. Does any of this sound familiar to you? Or maybe you grew up in a calm and stable environment, and that's helped you feel more resilient in the face of stress. The point is, our environments leave lasting imprints on us. So, when you think about how you respond to stress or difficult situations now, can you see any connections to the way you grew up? Sometimes, the ways we learned to cope back then stick with us into adulthood, even when we don't realize it.

And then there are your **life experiences.** This one's a biggie. Have you ever reacted to something and thought, "Why did I get so upset over that?" Sometimes, our reactions aren't really about the present moment—they're about something deeper, something from the past. Life experiences, especially traumatic ones, can leave emotional scars that don't just fade away. Even when you think you've moved on, your brain might still be holding on to the memory, reacting as if the danger is still there. Maybe there was a time in your life when you went through something really difficult—an event or series of events that left a mark. Your brain likely developed coping mechanisms to help you get through that time, but now those same mechanisms might not be serving you so well. For instance, if you experienced a lot of loss, maybe your mind learned to protect you by numbing your emotions, making it hard to feel joy or connection. Have you noticed that certain situations trigger an emotional response that seems out of proportion? That's often your brain's way of signaling that there's something deeper going on, something tied to past experiences that's still influencing your mental health today.

It's important to remember that talking about these root causes—genetics, environment, and life experiences—isn't about blaming yourself or anyone else. It's about gaining a clearer understanding of what's shaping your mental health. The more you can connect these dots, the more you'll feel empowered to take steps toward healing. So, as you think about your own journey, have you started to see some patterns or connections between your past and the way you feel today? Maybe understanding where these feelings come from is already giving you a bit more clarity. And that's the first step toward making real changes.

End of Chapter Reflection

Self-discovery is an ongoing journey, and the fact that you're here, taking these steps, already shows how committed you are to understanding your mental health. We've explored some of the most common mental health challenges—anxiety, depression, low self-esteem, and trauma—and hopefully, you've started to see how they might be showing up in your own life. It's not always easy to face these struggles head-on, is it? But here's the important thing: you're not in this alone. Everyone carries their own set of battles, and what truly matters is that you've chosen to face yours.

You've also begun to uncover the deeper roots of these challenges. Whether it's genetics, the environment you grew up in, or significant life experiences, these factors all contribute to how you feel today. It's empowering, isn't it, to realize that your feelings don't define you? They're just one part of your larger story. And by identifying where these emotions and struggles come from, you've already taken the first steps toward healing. Each piece of the puzzle you've uncovered brings you closer to greater self-awareness.

Now that you've gained this insight, it's time to apply it. Understanding your struggles is powerful, but taking action is what will truly make the difference. Over the next week, I invite you to embark on a 7-day challenge, designed to help you put your newfound understanding into practice. Each day, you'll focus on different aspects of your mental health, with practical exercises and thoughtful prompts to guide you along the way. Let's take this insight and turn it into meaningful growth together:

Day 1: Journal about your emotions today. Take note of any patterns in your feelings—are you experiencing stress, sadness, or worry? Reflect on when and why these emotions tend to appear.

Day 2: Complete a mood tracker for the day. Observe how your mental health fluctuates and what triggers certain moods. Were there any specific events or interactions that changed how you felt?

Day 3: Identify one major stressor in your life and list the ways it affects your mental well-being. How has this stressor impacted your emotions, thoughts, and relationships? Think of one small action you can take to manage it.

Day 4: Practice mindfulness for 10 minutes today. Focus on your thoughts and feelings in the present moment. Are there any recurring worries or thoughts that stand out? Write them down after your session.

Day 5: Reflect on a past experience that still affects you today. How does it show up in your life? Write a letter to your past self, offering understanding and support for the feelings you've carried with you.

Day 6: Spend time today connecting with someone who brings positivity into your life. Observe how this interaction impacts your mood and overall mental health. Journal about the experience.

Day 7: Look back over your week and review your journal entries and mood tracker. What patterns have emerged? Are there any connections between your emotions and the situations you faced? Identify one strategy to continue practicing going forward.

As you wrap up this week of self-reflection and exploration, consider what it means to truly understand your struggles. How has your perception of your mental health changed? What have you discovered about yourself that you didn't realize before? The more you know about your mental health, the better equipped you'll be to make meaningful changes.

But understanding your struggles is only one part of the equation. There's another layer that often holds people back—the stigma surrounding mental health. Have you ever hesitated to talk about your struggles because you feared judgment? Or maybe you've noticed how others shy away from sharing their experiences. Why is it that mental health issues still carry such stigma, even when they're so common? This is something worth exploring deeper.

Chapter 3: The Stigma of Mental Health

"Shame is the lie someone told you about yourself." — Anais Nin.

Let's talk about stigma. It's a word that carries a lot of weight, especially when it comes to mental health. But what exactly does it mean? Stigma, at its core, is a mark of shame or disgrace that society places on someone due to a particular characteristic or condition. When we talk about mental health stigma, we're referring to the judgments, assumptions, and misunderstandings people often face when they struggle with mental health challenges. Have you ever felt like your mental health struggles are something to hide? Like if you opened up about them, people might see you differently? That's the power of stigma—it creates a sense of "otherness," a separation that makes you feel like your struggles are something to be ashamed of, when in reality, they're a part of the human experience.

Stigma can be subtle, yet its impact is anything but. It affects how people perceive themselves and how they believe others see them. Imagine carrying the weight of anxiety or depression, and on top of that, feeling like you have to hide it because you fear being judged or misunderstood. It's exhausting, isn't it? Stigma doesn't just affect how you see yourself; it also influences how willing you are to seek help. When you believe that reaching out will make you seem weak or incapable, you're far less likely to take that important step toward healing. Stigma convinces you to suffer in silence, making it harder to break free from the very struggles you're dealing with. So, if you've ever felt hesitant to talk about what you're going through because of how you think others will react, you're not alone. This is exactly what stigma does—it isolates you, making your mental health struggles feel like a secret you need to keep.

Personal and Societal Impact

Stigma has both personal and societal effects. On a personal level, it can lead to feelings of shame and harsh self-criticism. Have you ever caught yourself thinking that your mental health struggles are a sign of weakness? Maybe you've told yourself that you should "just snap out of it" or that your emotions aren't as serious as they seem. That's stigma talking. It thrives on making you believe that struggling with mental health somehow means you're flawed or inadequate, when in reality, mental health challenges are something we all face in one form or another. Think about it—how often have you been hard on yourself for feeling anxious, sad, or overwhelmed? Stigma convinces you that these feelings make you "less than" others, even though they're a normal part of being human.

This internalized stigma can lead to isolation. You start to believe that no one else could possibly understand what you're going through, or worse, that if you share your struggles, people will think less of you. So, instead of reaching out, you keep everything to yourself. The irony is that this self-imposed silence only makes things harder. The longer you carry these feelings inside, the heavier they become, almost like you're trying to juggle too many emotions at once without anyone noticing. Can you relate to that? Have you ever felt the pressure to keep quiet about your mental health because you were afraid of how others might react? It's exhausting, and that silence can amplify the shame over time, making it feel even more isolating.

Now, let's think about the bigger picture—the societal impact of stigma. Stigma doesn't just live within individuals; it shapes the way entire communities view mental health. People who haven't personally experienced mental health struggles might not fully understand what it's like, and that lack of understanding can lead to assumptions, misconceptions, or even outright dismissal of the real challenges others are facing. Have you ever felt judged or misunderstood by someone who didn't "get it" when you tried to open up about your mental health? This kind of misunderstanding creates a culture where seeking help is seen as a sign of weakness or failure, rather than a brave and essential step toward healing. It can feel like the entire community is sending the message that mental health issues are something to hide or ignore, rather than something to address head-on.

This societal reluctance only makes things harder. In many circles, even today, talking about mental health issues can feel like crossing an unspoken line. Have you noticed how people sometimes avoid the subject altogether or change the topic when mental health comes up? This avoidance sends a clear message: mental health struggles are something to be ashamed of or hidden away. But the truth is, mental health is just as important as physical health—if not more. Can you imagine telling someone to ignore a broken leg or a persistent cough? Of course not! Yet, stigma pushes the idea that mental health issues should be swept under the rug, as if they'll magically disappear on their own.

The impact of this societal stigma is profound. It doesn't just discourage individuals from seeking help—it creates a ripple effect. When communities perpetuate the idea that mental health struggles are something to hide, it makes it harder for people to come forward, even when they desperately need support. The cycle continues, with individuals feeling more isolated, more ashamed, and less likely to reach out. And the more this happens, the more stigma grows, making it even harder to break free.

So, think about how this dynamic might be affecting you. Have there been moments when you wanted to speak up but held back because you feared being judged? Or maybe you've noticed how the people around you react when someone mentions mental health—do they brush it off, or do they show compassion and understanding? These societal cues shape how we view mental health, but the good news is that by recognizing them, we can start to change the way we think and talk about mental health—both personally and as a community.

Overcoming Stigma

So, how do you combat something as deeply ingrained as stigma? It starts with you, with the thoughts and beliefs that stigma has planted within your mind. The first step is to challenge those beliefs head-on. Have you ever taken a moment to really ask yourself why you feel ashamed or embarrassed about your mental health struggles? Is it because of what you've been told, or how society has portrayed people who struggle with their mental health? These thoughts can be so deeply ingrained that we often don't even realize they're shaping how we feel about ourselves. But questioning them is crucial. Why should you feel shame for something as natural as mental health struggles? Just as you wouldn't blame yourself for catching a cold, there's no reason to feel embarrassed about having moments of anxiety, depression, or any other mental health challenge.

Recognizing that your emotions are valid is a game-changer. You have the right to feel whatever you're feeling, without judgment or shame. Have you ever noticed how freeing it is when you give yourself permission to just *be*? That's the first step toward dismantling stigma from within. Understanding that your struggles don't define you—that they are only one part of your overall experience—helps you begin to break down that internalized stigma. It's about embracing the idea that mental health is a part of life, not something that makes you any less worthy or capable. Can you start to see how powerful that shift in thinking could be? When you stop letting stigma control how you view yourself, you're already well on your way to overcoming it.

But it doesn't stop with you. Then there's the community around you. We don't live in isolation, and the way others perceive mental health affects all of us. One of the most effective ways to combat stigma is by simply talking about it. By openly discussing mental health and sharing your experiences, you're helping to dismantle the barriers that stigma builds. Think about it—each time someone speaks up about their mental health journey, it creates space for others to do the same. Vulnerability has a way of opening doors, doesn't it? Maybe you've noticed that when a friend, family member, or even a public figure talks about their mental health, it makes you feel less alone. It's a reminder that struggling doesn't make you different—it makes you human. The more open we are, the more we normalize these conversations, and that alone has the power to chip away at stigma.

Have you ever considered how sharing your own story might help others? It's not just about your healing—it's about creating a ripple effect. When you're open about what you're going through, you give others permission to be open too. You're showing them that there's no shame in seeking support and that mental health challenges are nothing to be hidden or embarrassed about. It's the kind of openness that can inspire others to seek the help they need, knowing they're not alone in their struggles. And isn't that what we all want? To feel seen, heard, and understood, without judgment?

Beyond personal efforts, societal change is key. It starts with education. Communities need to understand what mental health really looks like—how common it is, how it affects everyday people, and why it's just as important as physical health. Have you ever thought about how much misinformation there is about mental health? People who haven't personally experienced these struggles might not fully understand them, and that's where education comes in. We can change the way people think about mental health by fostering conversations that are open, honest, and free of judgment. So, what role can you play in this change? It might be as simple as starting a conversation with a loved one or supporting initiatives that aim to raise awareness and educate others about mental health.

Every small step counts when it comes to overcoming stigma. It's not always about making huge, sweeping changes—sometimes, it's the little things that make the biggest difference. Maybe you can be the one to shift the dialogue in your social circle, or perhaps you'll decide to support a mental health campaign in your community. Whatever you choose, know that you're contributing to a larger movement. Being part of that change, you help create a world where people can seek help without fear or shame. A world where mental health is treated with the same respect as physical health, and where no one has to feel like they're facing their struggles alone.

End of Chapter Reflection

Stigma has a way of silently weighing you down, convincing you that your mental health struggles are something to keep hidden. It plants the idea that admitting to these challenges makes you vulnerable or weak, but the truth is, acknowledging them is one of the bravest things you can do. Struggling with mental health doesn't make you less—it makes you human. Throughout this chapter, you've gained a clearer understanding of what stigma is and how it can foster feelings of shame, isolation, and hesitation to seek support. But more importantly, you've also explored ways to begin breaking free from these barriers within yourself and the world around you.

Recognizing the impact of stigma is a crucial part of reclaiming your mental health and moving toward a more open, authentic way of living. It's not just about understanding stigma intellectually; it's about taking steps to dismantle it, piece by piece. Whether it's challenging the beliefs that have taken root in your mind or contributing to a larger conversation in your community, you now have the tools to push back against stigma.

With this newfound clarity, it's time to put that knowledge into action. The exercises below are designed to help you reflect on how stigma has shown up in your life and to start actively challenging it. As you work through them, remember that each step you take—no matter how small—brings you closer to a place of greater self-acceptance and freedom:

Journaling Your Experience with Stigma
Take some time to write about a moment when you felt judged or ashamed because of your mental health struggles. How did it affect you? What thoughts did you have about yourself in that moment? By getting these feelings out on paper, you can start to untangle the negative beliefs you may have internalized.

Reframing Negative Thoughts
Think about a specific negative belief you have about yourself related to your mental health (e.g., "I'm weak for feeling this way"). Now, challenge that belief by writing down evidence that proves it wrong. For example, remind yourself of times when you've shown strength by seeking help or coping with tough situations.

Having an Honest Conversation
Choose someone you trust and have an open conversation about your mental health. Share your struggles and ask about theirs. You might be surprised at how connecting on this level can reduce feelings of shame and isolation for both of you.

Supporting Others
Reflect on how you can be more supportive of others in their mental health journey. What can you do to reduce stigma within your community or social circle? This could involve educating others, being more open about your own experiences, or simply being a good listener.

Daily Affirmations to Combat Stigma
Each day, write or say a positive affirmation that challenges the stigma you've faced. For example, "My struggles don't define me," or "Seeking help shows

strength." Repeating these affirmations can help you rewire the negative thoughts stigma has planted.

As you continue exploring your mental health, take a moment to reflect on how stigma has influenced your willingness to address your struggles. Has it ever made you hesitate to reach out for help? What beliefs about mental health have you been holding onto, and are they truly based in reality? These are important questions to keep in mind as you move forward on this journey.

Our next discussion will explore specific mental health challenges, starting with anxiety. You'll discover how understanding the nuances of these struggles can provide you with greater clarity. Anxiety, for instance, shows up in different ways. Do you notice how your body sometimes reacts before your mind even processes the anxiety? Or how something small can trigger spiraling thoughts? We'll take a closer look at how anxiety shows up, the ways it can grip your mind and body, and the strategies you can use to handle it more effectively.

PART 2:
STRATEGIES FOR SPECIFIC MENTAL HEALTH CHALLENGES

Chapter 4: Conquering Anxiety

"If you want to conquer the anxiety of life, live in the moment, live in the breath." — Amit Ray.

Anxiety can feel overwhelming, can't it? It sneaks into your thoughts, making your heart race, your palms sweat, and sending your mind into a spiral of worry over things that haven't even happened yet. But what is anxiety, really? At its core, anxiety is your body's natural way of responding to stress. It's that feeling of fear or unease about the future that we all experience from time to time. But when it becomes too much—starts interfering with your everyday life—that's when it can feel more like a burden than a passing feeling.

You might notice anxiety showing up in a few different ways. Maybe it's those racing thoughts that won't quit, or the constant worrying that keeps you up at night. Sometimes, it even takes a physical toll—headaches, an upset stomach, or that tense feeling in your chest. Have you ever found yourself stuck in a cycle of "what ifs," playing out every worst-case scenario in your mind, even though you know most of them won't happen? That's anxiety pulling you away from the present moment, drawing your focus into the unknown and filling it with fear.

But here's the good news: anxiety doesn't have to run your life. It can be managed, and you can regain control with the right tools and strategies. Let's walk through some of the ways you can take charge of anxiety and bring yourself back to a place of calm.

Mindfulness Techniques

One of the most powerful tools for managing anxiety is mindfulness. Mindfulness is all about staying grounded in the present moment, focusing on what's happening right now rather than getting lost in anxious thoughts about the future. Practicing mindfulness regularly teaches your brain to respond more calmly to stress and anxiety triggers. Let's explore a few mindfulness techniques that can help you manage anxiety:

- **Deep Breathing**: When anxiety hits, your breathing often becomes shallow and fast, which only adds to the feeling of panic. Deep breathing exercises can help slow your heart rate and calm your mind. Try this: Sit comfortably, close your eyes, and take a slow, deep breath in through your nose, counting to four. Hold the breath for a count of four, then slowly exhale through your mouth for a count of four. Repeat this several times, focusing on the sensation of your breath entering and leaving your body. Do you feel a little more centered?

- **Progressive Muscle Relaxation**: Anxiety can cause physical tension in your body, sometimes without you even realizing it. Progressive muscle relaxation is a technique that helps release that tension, one muscle group at a time. Start by tensing the muscles in your feet, holding for a few seconds, then relaxing them. Move up through your body—legs, stomach, arms, shoulders—tensing and relaxing each muscle group. By the time you've worked through your body, you'll likely feel much more relaxed.

- **Mindful Meditation**: Meditation is a powerful way to train your mind to stay present. Set aside just five or ten minutes a day to sit quietly and focus on your breath. If your mind starts to wander, gently bring your attention back to your breathing. Over time, this practice can help reduce the frequency and intensity of anxious thoughts.

Cognitive-Behavioral Strategies

While mindfulness helps you stay grounded in the moment, cognitive-behavioral techniques focus on changing the way you think. Cognitive-behavioral therapy (CBT) is a proven approach to managing anxiety, helping you identify and challenge the negative thought patterns that fuel it. Let's explore some of the key techniques from CBT:

- **Reframing Negative Thoughts**: When anxiety strikes, your mind often latches onto the worst-case scenarios, creating a cycle of fear and worry. Reframing is about taking those anxious thoughts and viewing them through a more balanced, realistic lens. For example, let's say you're preparing for a big presentation and the thought pops into your head: "I'm going to completely mess this up." Instead of letting that thought spiral, you can stop and challenge it by asking yourself: "What evidence do I have that I'll fail?" or "What are the chances I'll do well, given that I've prepared?" Reframing teaches your mind to recognize when it's overreacting and helps you shift toward more constructive thinking. Over time, this practice reduces the power of anxiety by putting your thoughts into perspective. The more you reframe, the more you'll start to break the habit of catastrophic thinking and build a habit of thinking more logically and calmly.

- **Exposure Therapy**: Anxiety often pushes you to avoid things that make you uncomfortable. It could be anything from social interactions to certain tasks at work, but the more you avoid them, the stronger your anxiety becomes around those situations. Exposure therapy works by gradually introducing you to your fears, one small step at a time, so that you become less sensitive to them. Think of it like slowly dipping your toes into cold water until you're comfortable enough to dive in. For example, if social situations make you anxious, you might start by practicing conversations with a close friend or in a small group setting. Once that feels manageable, you could take the next step by attending a larger event. The goal is to face your fears in a controlled way so that over time, they lose their hold on you. It's not about forcing yourself into overwhelming situations but about building up your tolerance at a pace that feels doable.

- **Problem-Solving Skills**: Anxiety can make you feel like even the smallest issues are insurmountable problems. You might feel overwhelmed, unsure of where to start, or paralyzed by indecision. Learning problem-solving skills helps you break down challenges into smaller, more manageable pieces. For instance, instead of getting stuck in the anxiety of "I have too much work to do," you can break that thought down into actionable steps: "What do I need to do first? What can wait until later?" Start by identifying the specific issue causing your anxiety, then brainstorm possible solutions. Once you have a few options, decide on the best course of action and take it one step at a time. Problem-solving gives you a sense of control and makes what initially felt overwhelming much more manageable. It helps you shift from feeling powerless to proactive, which is crucial for reducing anxiety.

Lifestyle Modifications

Beyond mindfulness and cognitive-behavioral techniques, sometimes the simplest changes in your daily routine can make a huge difference in managing anxiety. You might be surprised at how much the way you eat, how often you move, and how well you sleep impact your mental well-being. Have you ever stopped to think about how your lifestyle might be contributing to your anxiety or perhaps easing it without you even realizing it?

Let's start with diet. Have you ever noticed how certain foods can really affect your mood? Maybe after a heavy, sugary meal, you feel sluggish or irritable. On the other hand, when you eat something light and nutritious, you might feel more energized and balanced. It's not just about avoiding "junk food"; it's about fueling your body in a way that supports your mental health too. Eating a balanced diet rich in fruits, vegetables, whole grains, and lean proteins can help stabilize your energy levels throughout the day. When your body feels good, your mind tends to follow. And let's talk about caffeine and sugar. Have you noticed how that morning coffee might make your heart race a bit too fast, or how a sugary snack in the afternoon leaves you jittery? Cutting back on these can prevent those spikes in anxiety and help you feel more centered. It's a small adjustment, but the impact can be significant.

Now, think about exercise. You don't have to run marathons or spend hours in the gym to feel the benefits. Physical activity, even in small amounts, is one of the best ways to relieve anxiety naturally. When you move, your body releases endorphins, those wonderful chemicals that boost your mood and help you feel more at ease. Have you ever noticed how a simple walk outside can help clear your mind? Or maybe you've felt the calm that comes after a good workout. Even if it's just a few minutes of stretching or a leisurely stroll around the block, getting your body moving is like hitting a mental reset button. And the best part? The effects are often immediate—you feel that sense of relief right away, and it helps you sleep better, manage stress, and stay more grounded.

Speaking of sleep, it's no secret that anxiety and sleep problems often go hand in hand. When you're anxious, it can be hard to fall asleep or stay asleep. Your mind might race, replaying the day's worries or anticipating tomorrow's challenges. But here's the thing: sleep is one of the most important things you can prioritize for your mental health. Creating a calming bedtime routine can make all the difference. Have you tried turning off your screens an hour before bed? The blue light from phones and computers can trick your brain into staying alert, making it harder to wind down. Or maybe you've experimented with relaxation exercises, like reading something calming, practicing deep breathing, or listening to soothing music before you fall asleep. These small habits can help signal to your body that it's time to relax, leading to a deeper, more restorative sleep. Over time, improving your sleep quality can greatly reduce your anxiety levels, making it easier to handle stress during the day.

These lifestyle modifications might seem simple, but they're incredibly powerful tools in managing anxiety. When you nourish your body, keep it active, and give it the rest it needs, you're also giving your mind the support it deserves. So, take a moment to reflect—what changes could you start making today to better care for your mental health? Little by little, these adjustments can make a world of difference.

End of Chapter Reflection

Anxiety is something that touches so many aspects of life, and it often feels overwhelming. But as you've explored here, anxiety doesn't have to control you. You've learned what anxiety is, how it manifests, and the variety of tools available to manage it—mindfulness techniques that bring you back to the present, cognitive-behavioral strategies that reshape how you think, and lifestyle changes that support your mental and physical well-being. The key takeaway is that anxiety, while powerful, is something you can learn to navigate. Each small step you take builds toward a calmer, more centered version of yourself.

Now that you've gained this knowledge, it's time to put it into practice. The exercises below are designed to help you apply what you've learned and deepen your understanding of how anxiety affects you personally. Take your time with each one and notice how your mind and body respond:

Daily Deep Breathing Practice
Set aside five minutes each day to practice deep breathing. Notice how your body and mind feel before and after the exercise. Write down any changes in your mood or energy levels.

Track Your Triggers
For one week, keep a journal of moments when you feel anxious. What was happening in the lead-up to those feelings? Were there specific triggers or patterns? Reviewing this journal can help you identify common anxiety sources in your life.

Challenge a Negative Thought
The next time you notice a negative, anxious thought, challenge it. Write down the thought and then reframe it with a more balanced perspective. Notice how this shift affects your anxiety levels.

Mindful Meditation Routine
Incorporate a short mindful meditation session into your daily routine. Start with just five minutes and gradually increase the time as you become more comfortable with the practice. Reflect on how staying present helps calm your mind.

Set a Sleep Routine
Commit to a sleep routine that promotes relaxation. Turn off screens an hour before bed, avoid heavy meals late at night, and try a short relaxation exercise before sleep. Track how these changes impact both your anxiety and your quality of rest.

As you move forward, think about the ways anxiety has affected your daily life. Have you noticed any patterns in your thoughts or behaviors that seem tied to it? Now that you've explored anxiety in depth, you'll be better prepared to manage these feelings when they arise.

And as we continue our journey, we'll shift our focus to another major mental health challenge: depression. Depression often feels like a weight that's hard to lift, making even the simplest tasks feel monumental. Have you ever wondered why some days seem heavier than others, or why joy feels so far out of reach? We'll explore what depression feels like, how it impacts your life, and most importantly, the steps you can take toward healing.

Chapter 5: Overcoming Depression

"Even when you feel hopeless, you can still move forward, step by step, even if it's just a small step." — Sheryl Sandberg.

Have you ever felt like you're drowning, but everyone else around you is breathing just fine? Like you're carrying an invisible weight on your shoulders that no one else can see? Depression can feel exactly like that—a heavy, persistent cloud that makes even the simplest tasks seem impossible. But you're not alone. In fact, did you know that over **264 million people** worldwide experience depression, according to the World Health Organization? That's millions of people, just like you, struggling to find their way through the darkness. And yet, even in the middle of that struggle, there is hope.

Depression can make you feel stuck, as though joy, energy, and motivation are out of reach. But here's the truth: no matter how overwhelming it feels right now, there's always a way forward. It might be slow and not feel like progress at first, but each small step you take is a step toward healing. So, let's explore depression together—not just the weight of it, but the reasons behind it, how it shows up in your life, and what you can do to start moving toward a lighter place.

Causes of Depression

Depression doesn't just appear out of nowhere, does it? Have you ever found yourself wondering, *Why do I feel like this?* It can be confusing, especially when it feels like your mood takes a nosedive for no obvious reason. But the truth is, depression often has deep, complex roots, and while it's not always easy to pinpoint exactly where it comes from, understanding the potential causes can help you make sense of your experience. Let's talk about some of the most common reasons depression takes hold.

For some people, depression has a **genetic** side to it. Have you ever noticed patterns of mental health struggles within your family? If so, it's possible that certain genes might make you more prone to feeling this way. But don't let that thought discourage you—it doesn't mean you're stuck in this place forever. Think of it this way: just as eye color or height runs in families, so too can mental health vulnerabilities. Knowing that genetics might play a role can take away some of the guilt or self-blame you might be carrying. Depression isn't a flaw in your character; it's just one piece of a bigger picture that's influenced by so many things.

Then, there's the impact of **life experiences**. Have you gone through something that shook you to your core? Sometimes, it's those big, painful events—losing someone you love, experiencing abuse, or going through a major life transition—that can trigger depression. These experiences often leave scars, not the kind you can see, but the kind that stay hidden inside. Have you ever found that certain memories or situations can bring those old feelings of sadness or helplessness rushing back? That's trauma lingering in the background, sometimes long after the event itself has passed. The weight of those past experiences can sneak up on you and contribute to feelings of depression without you even realizing it.

Let's not forget about **stress**. Have you ever felt like life was just too much to handle, like you're carrying a load that keeps getting heavier no matter how hard you try to lighten it? Long-term stress—from work, relationships, finances, or anything else—can slowly chip away at your emotional reserves until there's not much left. It's that feeling of being on edge, like you're running on fumes but there's no time to refuel. Have you been there? Where you just can't seem to catch a break, and eventually, your mind and body can't keep up with the demands being placed on you. That's when stress can spiral into depression, leaving you feeling drained, exhausted, and overwhelmed by even the smallest tasks.

And then there are the **chemical imbalances** in the brain. Depression is often linked to a shortage of certain neurotransmitters, like serotonin, which helps regulate your mood. When these chemicals are out of balance, it's not something you can just will away—it's a real, physical condition. Have you ever heard someone say, *Just snap out of it?* If only it were that simple, right? When your brain's chemistry is off, it affects not only how you feel emotionally, but also how your body functions physically. This imbalance is a reminder that depression is as real as any physical illness—it's not "all in your head." Knowing this can help you recognize that what you're going through is valid, and it's something you can work through with the right support.

Symptoms of Depression

Now, let's talk about the ways depression can show up in your life. It doesn't always look the same for everyone—sometimes it creeps in slowly, and other times it hits like a wave of emotions you can't escape. One of the most common feelings associated with depression is that heavy sense of dread, like you're stuck in place with no way out. It's that feeling of being weighed down by an emotional burden you can't lift, no matter how hard you try.

Feelings of **hopelessness** are often at the heart of depression. You may find yourself believing that things will never improve, that there's no point in trying anymore. These thoughts can be persistent and overwhelming, making everything in your life feel dark and unchangeable. But it's important to remember that as real as those feelings are, they don't reflect the full picture—they're the voice of depression telling you that hope is out of reach, even when it's not.

Another common symptom is **fatigue and a lack of energy**. Depression doesn't just weigh on your mind; it saps your physical strength too. Even the smallest tasks—like getting out of bed or making a simple decision—can feel exhausting. You might feel worn out, even if you haven't done much of anything. That's depression working behind the scenes, draining both your body and your mind, making it harder to engage with the world around you.

Changes in appetite and sleep patterns often go hand in hand with depression. You might find yourself eating more than usual, looking for comfort in food, or maybe you lose your appetite altogether, feeling like eating is just too much effort. Sleep can become a struggle too—you might be lying awake for hours, unable to quiet your mind, or sleeping for long stretches just to escape the heaviness of your emotions. These physical changes are part of how depression affects your body as much as your thoughts.

You may also notice that concentrating becomes a challenge. Tasks that were once easy or enjoyable now feel overwhelming or out of reach. Simple decisions might suddenly feel monumental, and you might be unable to focus on even the things you used to love. It's not a matter of laziness or a lack of motivation—it's your mind trying to cope with the fog that depression creates.

And finally, one of the most noticeable signs of depression is the **loss of interest** in activities that once brought you joy. The hobbies, social events, or even people that used to light up your day now feel distant, almost irrelevant. It's as if the spark that used to bring color to your world has been dimmed, leaving you feeling disconnected and numb. That's depression pulling you away from the things that once made you feel alive, but remember, even that disconnection isn't permanent.

Types of Depression

Depression isn't one-size-fits-all. It shows up in different ways, and sometimes it can be confusing to understand why your symptoms fluctuate or why some days feel so drastically different from others. That's because depression has many faces, each with its own unique impact on how you feel and navigate daily life. Let's break down some of the most common types, so you can start to understand what you might be experiencing more clearly:

- **Major Depressive Disorder (MDD)**
  Major Depressive Disorder is a classic form of depression that brings intense feelings of sadness, hopelessness, and disinterest in things that once brought joy. Have you ever felt like a dark cloud has settled over your mind, blocking out any sense of happiness or motivation? With MDD, these feelings can last for weeks or even months, making it hard to imagine things ever getting better. You might find yourself withdrawing from loved ones, losing interest in hobbies, or even struggling to get out of bed in the morning. It's as if the weight of the world has settled on your shoulders, and you're left wondering if you'll ever feel "normal" again. But even in the darkest times, there are ways to begin the healing process, one step at a time.

- **Persistent Depressive Disorder (PDD)**
  Have you ever felt like you're just coasting through life, not fully present or engaged, but not completely overwhelmed either? That's how Persistent Depressive Disorder (also known as dysthymia) can feel. It's a long-term, low-grade form of depression that lingers in the background, casting a shadow over your daily experiences. You may not experience the extreme lows of Major Depression, but the constant sense of sadness or emptiness can make life feel dull and colorless. Days blur together, and even though you're functioning, you might feel disconnected from the joy and excitement that others seem

to find so easily. PDD can last for years, creating a sense of numbness that's hard to shake. It's like living under a gray sky, where the sun never fully breaks through.

- **Seasonal Affective Disorder (SAD)**
Do you ever notice your mood shifting when the seasons change, especially when the days grow shorter and the sunlight becomes scarce? If so, you're not alone. Seasonal Affective Disorder (SAD) is a type of depression triggered by changes in the seasons, typically during fall and winter. The lack of sunlight during these months can disrupt your body's internal clock and lower serotonin levels, which affects your mood. SAD often brings feelings of fatigue, lethargy, and sadness, making it hard to find motivation or energy. You might find yourself wanting to sleep more, eat more, or withdraw from social activities. It's as if the cold weather and dark skies seep into your emotional state, making everything feel a little heavier. The good news? Understanding the seasonal pattern can help you take proactive steps to manage these feelings and prepare for the months when SAD tends to strike.

- **Bipolar Disorder**
Depression doesn't always stay in one place—it can swing between extreme highs and crushing lows, which is what happens in Bipolar Disorder. Have you ever felt like you're on top of the world one day, only to crash into the depths of despair the next? That's the hallmark of Bipolar Disorder, where periods of mania (intense energy, euphoria, and impulsivity) are followed by episodes of deep depression. The highs can make you feel invincible, driving you to take risks or make decisions you wouldn't normally consider. But when the depression hits, it's as though all that energy is drained from your body, leaving you exhausted and emotionally worn out. This constant back-and-forth can be confusing and exhausting for you and the people around you. Learning how to manage the

swings between mania and depression is key to finding balance and stability.

Creating Routines

One of the simplest but most powerful steps toward moving through depression is by establishing routines. I know that might sound daunting, especially when getting out of bed itself can feel like an enormous accomplishment. But routines offer more than just a plan for your day—they provide a sense of stability and structure when everything else feels overwhelming and chaotic. Depression often thrives in uncertainty, and when your days lack structure, it can intensify that feeling of being lost or stuck. Have you ever noticed how much more challenging everything feels when you don't have a clear idea of what's next? That's where routines can make a difference—they create a framework that helps you feel a little more grounded, even in the toughest moments.

The key is to start small. You don't need to map out a complicated, tightly packed schedule, especially when just getting through the day feels hard. In fact, trying to create a rigid routine all at once can sometimes lead to more frustration. Instead, focus on one or two simple, achievable habits. It might be something as straightforward as waking up at the same time each morning, regardless of how you feel, or having a consistent breakfast. These small actions might not seem significant at first, but they lay the groundwork for more structure in your day.

Starting small is important because depression can drain your energy and make even the smallest task feel monumental. But here's the beauty of it: every tiny habit you establish builds momentum. You don't need to fill your entire day with activities right away; instead, start with what feels manageable. For example, setting aside just 10 minutes for a morning walk or stretching session can have a powerful impact. This simple habit gives your day a positive start and a sense of rhythm, even if the rest of the day feels heavy. It's not about perfection—it's about consistency and reminding yourself that even in the face of depression, you can take control of certain parts of your day.

Routines are like stepping stones. As you repeat these small habits, you begin to create a sense of accomplishment. Have you ever experienced that feeling of satisfaction after completing something small, like making your bed or washing the dishes? Even these little victories can offer a sense of achievement, which is especially important when depression makes everything feel like an uphill battle. Each small task completed is a reminder that you *can* move forward, even when it feels impossible.

Over time, these small routines start to add up. They form the foundation for recovery because they give you structure and consistency, which are key to regaining your sense of balance. When your mind is clouded by depression, it can be hard to see beyond the next hour, let alone the next day. Routines help create a gentle roadmap, something you can lean on when it feels like everything else is out of your control. And as these routines become part of your daily life, they make space for you to introduce more activities that support your well-being, like hobbies or social connections, all at your own pace.

It's important to remember that progress doesn't happen overnight, and that's okay. There will be days when sticking to a routine feels easier and days when it feels nearly impossible. The goal isn't to be perfect—it's to keep trying. Some days, just completing one small task might be all you can manage, and that's still a victory. By creating these routines, you're gradually building a framework that allows you to reclaim a sense of control over your life. Even when depression tries to pull you into isolation and inertia, these small, consistent actions remind you that you're capable of moving forward, step by step.

Finding Joy in Small Things

When you're dealing with depression, the idea of joy can feel distant, even unattainable. But what if you didn't have to find *big* joy right away? Sometimes, it's the small moments that start to bring light back into your life. Have you ever experienced a fleeting moment of peace while sipping your favorite tea, or a brief smile during a funny movie scene? These small pockets of joy are often overlooked, but they are there—waiting to be noticed.

One practice that helps is gratitude journaling. It doesn't have to be elaborate. Each day, write down one or two things, no matter how small, that brought a moment of peace or made you feel a little lighter. Maybe it was the warmth of the sun on your skin, or the sound of birds chirping outside your window. These small moments remind you that even in the midst of darkness, there are still glimpses of light. Over time, paying attention to these small joys can start to shift your focus, helping you see that joy isn't completely out of reach.

Engaging in hobbies or activities you once enjoyed is another way to start reconnecting with joy. It might feel forced at first, but sometimes just the act of doing can spark something inside you. Whether it's painting, reading, gardening, or even cooking, reintroducing activities that once made you happy can slowly bring back a sense of pleasure and purpose.

Positive Affirmations

Have you noticed how, during those tough moments, your own mind can sometimes become your harshest critic? That inner voice might tell you things like, "I'm not good enough," or "I'll never feel better." And when those thoughts settle in, they can feel overwhelmingly real, can't they? But here's something to remember: those thoughts don't have to control your narrative.

Positive affirmations are a way to gently push back against the negativity, replacing it with kinder, more compassionate self-talk.

Now, I know this might feel a bit strange at first. Positively talking to yourself, especially when you're not used to it, can seem awkward or even forced. But give it a try. Start by telling yourself simple, encouraging things like, "I am enough just as I am," or "I am worthy of love and happiness." It might feel uncomfortable at the beginning, but think of it as planting seeds. Over time, these affirmations begin to take root, gradually chipping away at the negativity that depression often brings.

Have you ever tried speaking kindly to yourself in moments of doubt? It can feel like a small step, but the more you practice, the more these positive affirmations build a mental shield—a protective layer between you and that harsh self-judgment. Each time you repeat an affirmation, you're reminding yourself that, no matter what depression tries to tell you, you are valuable, deserving of compassion, and capable of healing. It's a gentle but powerful way to reclaim control over your inner dialogue.

End of Chapter Reflection

Depression can often feel like an all-encompassing weight, but through understanding and small, deliberate steps, you've already begun to find ways to navigate through it. You've explored the many faces of depression, how it shows up in your life, and how tools like routines, finding joy in small moments, and practicing positive affirmations can help you regain a sense of control and hope. The key takeaway is this: while depression is a challenge, it doesn't define you. Even when it feels like everything is slipping away, there's always the possibility of moving forward—step by step. Progress doesn't have to be fast; even the smallest steps are a testament to your resilience and strength. Remember, you have the power to take those small steps toward healing, no matter how slow the journey feels.

To help you put these ideas into practice, I've created a 7-day challenge designed to reinforce the concepts you've explored. Each day focuses on a specific action or reflection to help you integrate these small but significant changes into your life. These tasks are gentle and doable—designed to offer support as you move forward.

- **Day 1: Morning Routine**
  Start your day with a simple morning routine. Choose a consistent wake-up time and add one small activity, like stretching, making your bed, or enjoying breakfast without distractions. Write down how establishing this routine makes you feel. Did it give you a sense of structure?

- **Day 2: Gratitude Practice**
  Take a moment today to write down three small things you're grateful for. It could be something as simple as the warmth of a cup of tea or the sound of rain outside your window. Pay attention to how this practice shifts your mindset, even if just a little.

- **Day 3: Reconnecting with an Activity**
  Revisit an activity or hobby you once enjoyed, even if it feels difficult at first. Whether it's reading, drawing, cooking, or something else, allow yourself to engage without expecting perfection. Reflect on how it feels to reconnect with this part of yourself.

- **Day 4: Positive Affirmations**
  Start your day by repeating two or three positive affirmations. Write them down and keep them close. Whenever a negative thought creeps in, gently counter it with one of your affirmations. By the end of the day, reflect on any changes in your self-talk and mood.

- **Day 5: Evening Reflection**
  As you wind down tonight, take a few minutes to reflect on your day. What small victories did you achieve today, no matter how minor they seem? Acknowledge them, write them down, and celebrate that progress, even if it feels small.

- **Day 6: Moving Your Body**
  Today, engage in some form of physical movement, whether it's a short walk, gentle stretching, or any other activity that feels good to you. Notice how your body feels before and after, and reflect on any changes in your mood or energy levels.

- **Day 7: Quiet Time**
  Set aside 10 minutes for quiet reflection or meditation. Let your mind rest without focusing on anything specific. Just observe your thoughts and feelings without judgment, and see how this simple act of quiet time impacts your mental state.

As you move through this 7-day challenge, take note of how these small, mindful actions begin to shape your mood and mindset. Even subtle shifts matter. What differences have you noticed in your energy, your thoughts, or your outlook on the day? Depression may sometimes feel like an uphill climb, but with each small step, you're building strength, resilience, and a deeper sense of self-awareness.

Looking ahead, we'll begin exploring a new layer of mental wellness: building self-confidence and self-esteem. These two are the foundation of how you see and value yourself. Have you ever wondered why some days you feel less sure of yourself, or why it's hard to trust in your abilities? Self-confidence and self-esteem often take a hit during tough times, but together, we'll dive into practical strategies to rebuild and strengthen them. Imagine what life could look like when you believe in your worth and trust in your abilities—let's start making that a reality.

Chapter 6: Building Self-Confidence and Self-Esteem

"Believe in yourself and all that you are. Know that there is something inside you that is greater than any obstacle." — Christian D. Larson.

Feeling confident and having a strong sense of self-worth aren't just qualities you're born with—they're things you develop over time. Think about how you feel when you trust yourself to make the right decisions, or when you truly believe you deserve happiness and respect. It changes how you show up in the world, doesn't it? Self-confidence and self-esteem influence so much of how you live your life, and when you start building them, you begin to feel more grounded in who you are and what you're capable of achieving.

Now, let's look at the differences between self-confidence and self-esteem, because while they often go hand in hand, they're not quite the same thing. Self-confidence is about trusting your abilities—knowing that you can handle whatever comes your way. It's that inner voice that tells you, "I've got this," even when you're stepping into something new or uncertain. Have you ever noticed how much easier it is to tackle challenges when you believe in your skills? That's self-confidence in action. But what about self-esteem? That runs a little deeper. Self-esteem is your overall sense of worth—how much you believe you deserve love, respect, and kindness. It's less about what you can *do* and more about who you *are* at your core.

The two work together. You can feel confident in your abilities but still struggle with self-esteem if you don't believe you deserve success or love. On the other hand, a strong sense of self-worth can help you weather failures or setbacks because deep down, you know those moments don't define your value. So, how do you strengthen both? By recognizing that you're not just capable of achieving great things—you're *worthy* of them too. When you find that balance between trusting your abilities and embracing your inherent worth, you'll start to move through life with a new sense of assurance. Step by step, you can build that solid foundation of both self-confidence and self-esteem.

Daily Confidence Boosters

Building self-confidence doesn't happen overnight, but there are small, actionable things you can do daily to give yourself a boost. Have you ever noticed how your posture or the way you carry yourself affects how you feel? Simply standing tall, making eye contact, and speaking clearly can shift how others perceive you—and, more importantly, how you perceive yourself. Practicing assertiveness is another great way to build confidence. Assertiveness doesn't mean being aggressive or forceful; it's about standing up for yourself with respect and clarity. Each time you express your needs or boundaries with confidence, you reinforce the belief that your voice matters.

Another confidence-building habit is stepping outside your comfort zone, even in small ways. Every time you push yourself to try something new, you're proving to yourself that you're capable. It could be as simple as speaking up in a meeting or learning a new skill—each success, no matter how small, becomes a brick in the foundation of your self-confidence. The more you practice these daily habits, the stronger your belief in yourself will become.

Challenging Negative Thoughts

Have you ever found yourself thinking, "I'm not good enough," or "I always mess things up"? These are classic examples of negative self-talk, and they can be incredibly damaging, slowly chipping away at both your self-confidence and self-esteem. It's easy to believe these thoughts when they pop up, especially if they've been hanging around for a long time. But here's the important truth: these thoughts are just that—*thoughts*. They aren't facts and don't define who you are. One of the most empowering things you can do is learn how to challenge these negative beliefs when they show up.

The first step is becoming aware of when these negative thoughts creep in. It's easy to let them slip by unnoticed because they've become such a natural part of your inner dialogue. But by actively paying attention, you can start to catch them in the moment. Have you ever stopped to ask yourself, "Is this thought really true?" or "What proof do I have that this thought is valid?" More often than not, you'll realize that these negative beliefs are rooted in fears or old insecurities rather than in actual evidence. For example, you might be telling yourself, "I always fail," but when you think about it, how many times have you succeeded? Chances are, your successes far outweigh your failures, but your mind has a way of amplifying the negative.

Once you start questioning these thoughts, you can begin to reframe them. Instead of letting "I'm not good enough" run on a loop in your mind, challenge it by saying, "I'm doing my best, and that's enough." Or, instead of, "I always mess things up," remind yourself, "I've made mistakes, but I learn and grow from them." By consistently replacing those harmful thoughts with more supportive and realistic ones, you'll begin to shift the narrative in your mind.

It's important to remember that this process doesn't happen overnight. Negative thoughts can be stubborn, especially if you've believed them for years. But each time you challenge and reframe them, you're weakening their hold on you. Over time, you'll find that these once automatic, critical thoughts show up less frequently, and when they do, they carry less weight. Instead, you'll start developing a more positive and empowering internal dialogue that supports your growth and helps you build self-confidence and self-esteem.

Imagine how freeing it would be to have an inner voice that says, "I am enough," or "I'm capable of learning and improving." This kind of thinking isn't about ignoring your flaws or pretending everything is perfect—it's about giving yourself the space to acknowledge your worth and see yourself for who you truly are, rather than through the lens of old fears or insecurities. Little by little, you'll begin to see just how powerful challenging these thoughts can be.

Self-Compassion Exercises

One of the most powerful ways to nurture your self-esteem is through practicing self-compassion. Think for a moment about how you treat a friend when they're going through a difficult time. You wouldn't criticize them or tell them they're not good enough, would you? No, you'd likely offer them kindness, support, and understanding. You'd listen, comfort them, and remind them of their worth. Now, imagine turning that same level of care inward, offering yourself the same compassion you so easily give to others. It might feel awkward or uncomfortable at first—after all, we tend to be our own harshest critics—but self-compassion is an essential practice for building and sustaining self-esteem.

So, let's start with this: have you ever taken a moment to forgive yourself for something that didn't go as planned? Maybe it was a mistake at work or a situation in your personal life that didn't unfold the way you hoped. We all have moments like these, where we find ourselves replaying events repeatedly, thinking, *If only I had done this differently*. But practicing self-forgiveness is about letting go of that self-blame. It doesn't mean excusing your actions or pretending the mistake didn't happen. Instead, it means accepting that you're human—and humans, by nature, are imperfect. We all stumble; what matters is how you choose to move forward.

Imagine the relief that comes from releasing yourself from the constant loop of self-criticism. It's like a weight lifting off your shoulders. By forgiving yourself, you're acknowledging that mistakes are part of growth. Think about it: how many times have you learned valuable lessons from a misstep? Instead of focusing on the failure, you can choose to see it as a learning opportunity. With self-compassion, you remind yourself that you are more than your mistakes, and those moments don't define your worth.

Another important aspect of self-compassion is accepting yourself, flaws and all. Let's be honest—everyone has things they wish to change about themselves. Maybe you're not as confident in certain situations, or perhaps you're hard on yourself about your appearance or abilities. But here's the truth: the things that make you different are often the very things that make you unique and valuable. Have you ever thought about celebrating those differences, rather than seeing them as shortcomings? When you practice self-compassion, you start to shift your focus away from what you perceive as imperfections and toward the qualities that make you who you are.

Take a moment to consider this: how often do you look in the mirror and speak kindly to yourself? How often do you acknowledge the things you've done well, rather than zeroing in on what you think went wrong? Self-compassion is about shifting that inner dialogue. Instead of focusing on what you didn't do or what you think is lacking, start to remind yourself of the things you've accomplished, the strengths you possess, and the effort you put into everything you do. It's about giving yourself credit where it's due and recognizing that you are deserving of the same kindness and respect that you so freely offer others.

Every time you engage in self-compassion, whether through self-forgiveness or self-acceptance, you reinforce the belief that you are worthy of love, respect, and kindness—especially from yourself. And the more you practice, the more this mindset becomes second nature. You'll find that, over time, treating yourself with compassion starts to feel as natural as breathing. It's about recognizing that you're enough just as you are, flaws and all.

End of Chapter Reflection

Self-confidence and self-esteem are the pillars of a fulfilling, authentic life. As you've explored in this chapter, self-confidence enables you to trust in your abilities and face challenges with courage, while self-esteem reinforces your inherent worth, regardless of your achievements or circumstances. Together, these qualities form a powerful foundation that allows you to navigate life with resilience and self-assurance.

By incorporating daily confidence boosters, challenging negative thoughts, and embracing self-compassion, you've begun to learn practical tools that will help strengthen these areas. It's a gradual journey, but every small step brings you closer to feeling more secure in who you are and what you're capable of. The key is consistency, and with time, you'll notice these small actions building into a stronger, more empowered version of yourself.

To help you put these ideas into practice, here's a 7-day challenge that will guide you in integrating what you've learned. Each day focuses on nurturing both your self-confidence and self-esteem, allowing you to grow in these important areas:

- **Day 1: Posture and Presence**
  Start your day by paying attention to your posture. Stand tall, make eye contact, and speak clearly in every

interaction. At the end of the day, reflect on how these small shifts affected your confidence and mood.

- **Day 2: Small Wins**
Choose one task or challenge today that feels slightly outside your comfort zone. It could be speaking up, trying something new, or completing a project. Reflect on how it felt to face that challenge and what you learned from it.

- **Day 3: Challenging Negative Thoughts**
Throughout the day, notice any negative thoughts that arise about yourself. Write them down and challenge each one by asking, "Is this really true?" Replace it with a more positive or realistic thought. Reflect on how this reframing affects your mindset.

- **Day 4: Self-Compassion Practice**
Take a moment today to forgive yourself for any mistakes or shortcomings, no matter how small. Offer yourself the same kindness you would give a friend. Write down one thing you're proud of about yourself, no matter how simple it seems.

- **Day 5: Assertiveness Practice**
Practice being assertive in one situation today. Whether it's setting a boundary or expressing your opinion, focus on being clear and respectful. Reflect on how it felt to stand up for yourself.

- **Day 6: Positive Affirmations**
Begin your day with three positive affirmations about yourself. Throughout the day, whenever a negative thought arises, counter it with one of your affirmations. Reflect on any shifts in your self-talk.

- **Day 7: Celebrating Yourself**
End the week by celebrating something about yourself—whether it's an achievement, a strength, or simply how far

you've come. Reflect on how this acknowledgment feels and how it impacts your self-esteem.

As you continue this journey, pay attention to how these small practices impact your self-confidence and self-esteem. Have you noticed any changes in the way you speak to yourself or approach challenges? While these steps may seem small, each one is contributing to a stronger, more grounded sense of self.

Now, let me ask you this: Have you ever wondered why certain past experiences continue to affect how you feel or react, even long after they've happened? Trauma has a way of shaping your view of yourself and the world, often leaving deep emotional scars that linger. In the coming section, we'll dive into the effects of trauma on your mental health. More importantly, we'll explore how you can begin the healing process, taking those first steps toward reclaiming your peace and well-being.

Chapter 7: Healing from Trauma

"Out of suffering have emerged the strongest souls; the most massive characters are seared with scars." — Khalil Gibran.

Trauma leaves its mark, altering the way you experience yourself and the world around you. It can come from a single, life-altering event or build up over time, slowly weakening your sense of stability. Either way, its effects linger in your mental and emotional well-being. Yet, even when it feels heavy, healing is within reach. Trauma doesn't have to define you—it's your response and the growth that follows which truly shape who you are.

Types of Trauma

Trauma isn't a one-size-fits-all experience—it can take many forms, depending on what you've been through. What deeply affects one person might leave someone else feeling entirely different. Knowing about the various types of trauma can provide the clarity needed to make sense of your feelings, reactions, and memories. Recognizing the specific kind of trauma you've experienced is a key step in your journey toward healing. Let's explore some of the main types:

- **Acute Trauma**
  Acute trauma stems from a single, distressing event that leaves a lasting emotional impact. Imagine experiencing a sudden accident, losing someone you love unexpectedly, or facing a violent incident. These events hit hard, and your sense of safety can be shattered in an instant. You might notice that ever since that moment, certain places, sounds, or even smells trigger intense emotions—almost like

you're reliving the experience. It can make you feel vulnerable, as though the world has become unpredictable and unsafe. Acute trauma often makes you feel as if life will never return to normal, but recognizing that this event has left an emotional wound is the first step in starting to heal.

- **Chronic Trauma**
  Chronic trauma builds over time, often through repeated exposure to stressful or harmful situations. Think of situations like living in an environment of ongoing abuse, growing up in a home full of conflict, or even facing constant bullying. It's the kind of trauma that doesn't hit all at once but rather wears you down day by day, leaving you feeling trapped and unsafe. Have you ever felt like you're always on edge, as if you're waiting for the next bad thing to happen? That's how chronic trauma impacts you—it eats away at your sense of stability, making it hard to ever fully relax. Over time, you might find it difficult to trust people or feel truly at ease, even when the traumatic situation is over. But understanding that this slow buildup of stress has shaped your emotions is a key part of reclaiming your sense of peace.

- **Complex Trauma**
  Complex trauma occurs when you've experienced multiple traumatic events, often in situations where you were dependent on someone who should have protected you. This type of trauma is common in cases of childhood abuse, neglect, or prolonged domestic violence. It's particularly damaging because it affects not just how you see others but how you see yourself. Maybe you've noticed that you struggle with self-worth or have difficulty forming close relationships. This kind of trauma doesn't just hurt—it leaves deep scars on your identity, making you question your value and place in the world. Have you ever felt like you don't quite know who you are, or that the

world is somehow harsher toward you? That's the long-lasting impact of complex trauma. Acknowledging that these painful experiences have shaped how you see yourself is the first step toward healing those wounds.

Grounding Techniques

When you're faced with painful memories or overwhelming emotions tied to trauma, it can feel like you're being pulled into a whirlpool of distress, as if you're caught in a storm that you just can't escape. In moments like these, your body and mind seem to lose their sense of safety, and everything feels chaotic and overwhelming. The good news is, grounding techniques are simple but powerful tools that can help pull you out of that emotional spiral. They're designed to keep you anchored to the present moment, reminding you that you're in control, even when it feels like you aren't.

Imagine a time when your thoughts began to race uncontrollably, when it felt like you couldn't stop reliving a painful memory or you were overwhelmed by fear, anxiety, or sadness. Maybe you've been in a crowded space, and suddenly, something triggered a flood of emotions, making you feel disoriented. Grounding techniques step in at moments like these, helping you shift your focus from those distressing thoughts to the present, the here and now. When emotions threaten to take over, grounding brings you back to a place where you can breathe, regain your sense of control, and remind yourself that you're safe.

One effective grounding method is focusing on your physical surroundings—what you can see, hear, touch, smell, and even taste. It's about redirecting your attention from the internal storm to the external world around you. Let's say your mind begins to spiral into worry or fear. Take a moment to look around you and name five things you can see. It could be the color of the walls, a picture frame, or a plant nearby. Then, engage your other senses.

Feel the fabric of your clothing against your skin, notice the coolness or warmth of the air around you, or listen to the distant hum of traffic outside. These small observations may seem insignificant, but they're incredibly powerful. They serve as reminders that while your emotions are real and valid, the traumatic event is in the past, and you are grounded in the present.

Another grounding technique involves using your breath to calm the storm inside. Deep, steady breaths are a simple but highly effective way to bring your body back to a place of balance. Start by taking a slow breath in, counting to four as you fill your lungs, and then slowly exhale for a count of four. As you breathe, focus on the sensation of your chest rising and falling. Notice how your body responds to each breath. Do you feel your heart rate begin to slow down? Does the tension in your muscles start to ease up, even just a little? Focusing on your breath not only calms your body but also signals to your brain that you're safe, that the threat is no longer present, and that it's okay to relax. It's a reminder that, in this moment, you are in control of your own breathing, your own body, and your own space.

Sometimes, grounding might involve using physical objects to help bring you back to the present. Carrying something small, like a smooth stone or a piece of fabric with a texture you enjoy, can be helpful. When you feel triggered or overwhelmed, hold that object in your hand and focus on its texture, weight, and temperature. How does it feel against your skin? This small act can serve as a powerful reminder that, despite the intensity of your feelings, you are here in the present, in a safe space.

Grounding also extends to your movements. Have you ever noticed how being physically active can sometimes help shift your emotional state? Taking a walk, stretching, or even doing a small task like washing your hands with cold water can help snap you out of the emotional whirlpool and reconnect you to your body. When your mind starts to spiral, moving your body intentionally helps break the cycle of distress. You're essentially telling your brain, "I'm here, I'm safe, and I'm capable of moving forward."

Every time you practice grounding, you're retraining your brain. You're teaching it that, although the traumatic experience may still echo in your thoughts, it doesn't have the power to control you. You are here, now, and you are safe. The more you practice these techniques, the more natural they will feel, and the easier it will become to manage those overwhelming moments when they arise.

Grounding techniques are like a mental toolkit you carry with you everywhere. Whether in public or at home, you can use these tools to center yourself when emotions threaten to take over. The key is consistency. The more you use grounding, the more your body and mind will respond to these gentle reminders that you're in control, that you've got this, and that healing is possible.

The Power of Storytelling

There's something incredibly healing about sharing your story, isn't there? It's as though speaking your truth lifts a heavy burden you've been carrying for far too long. Have you ever felt that sense of relief after opening up to someone, even just a little? That's because storytelling has the power to free you from the silence trauma often forces upon you. Trauma has a way of stealing your voice, making you feel like what happened is too big, too painful, or too overwhelming to talk about. But by telling your story, you reclaim control. You're no longer just living through it; you're actively shaping how you relate to it.

Narrative therapy taps into this power, allowing you to tell your story in a way that helps you heal. It's not about rewriting history or pretending the trauma didn't happen. Instead, it's about reframing your experience, seeing it through a different lens. You're not erasing the pain, but you are shifting your perspective to acknowledge both the hurt and the strength it took to survive.

You're the author of your story, and while trauma might be a significant chapter, it's not the whole book. You hold the pen, and you get to decide how the rest of the story unfolds.

Think about a time when you felt silenced by your trauma. Maybe you felt too ashamed, too hurt, or even too afraid to talk about what happened. But what if, instead of bottling those feelings, you started sharing your story, little by little? Whether it's with a trusted friend, a therapist, or even just writing in a journal, each time you speak your truth, you're reclaiming a part of yourself that trauma tried to take away. It's not about having the perfect words or even telling the story in a linear way—it's about getting it out of your head and into the open, where you can begin to make sense of it.

Imagine being able to reframe a traumatic experience—not to change what happened, but to change how you see it. Let's say you went through a difficult situation where you felt powerless, like you had no control. In that moment, it may have seemed like you were entirely at the mercy of circumstances. But now, as you look back on it, can you also see the strength it took to get through it? Can you recognize the courage it took to keep going, even when it felt impossible? That's the power of reframing your story. It's about acknowledging the pain while also recognizing your resilience.

Each time you share your story, whether by writing it down or talking it through with someone you trust, you're reclaiming a piece of your narrative. You're not letting trauma write the final word. You're telling your story on your own terms, and that can be incredibly empowering. You might find that each time you speak about it, its weight gets just a little bit lighter. It's not that the pain disappears, but it becomes more manageable because you're no longer carrying it alone. Have you ever considered writing about your experiences or talking through them with someone? These small steps can be incredibly freeing, helping you to see your trauma as just one part of your story, rather than the whole thing.

And here's the beautiful thing about storytelling—it doesn't just help you. You might be surprised at how it resonates with others when you share your story. Sometimes, people who have been through similar experiences find comfort in hearing that they're not alone. Your story can become a bridge, connecting you with others who understand and support you. It's a reminder that, even in your darkest moments, there is light in the form of shared experiences and human connection.

As you begin to explore the idea of sharing your story, remember that you get to decide when and how it's told. There's no rush, no pressure. Whether you start by writing a single sentence in a journal or having a deep conversation with someone you trust, each step is a victory. Each word is a piece of your story that you're taking back from trauma. And with every bit you share, you move closer to healing.

Seeking Professional Help

There's a certain strength in knowing when it's time to reach out for help, isn't there? Sometimes, we carry the weight of our trauma for so long that asking for help feels like admitting defeat—but it's not. It's one of the bravest things you can do for yourself. Have you ever thought that talking through your trauma with someone could make a difference, but didn't quite know where to begin? You're not alone. So many people struggle with where to start when it comes to seeking professional help, but the truth is, healing doesn't have to be a solo journey.

There's real power in having a professional by your side—someone who's trained to understand the complexities of trauma, someone who can guide you through those difficult emotions. A therapist, counselor, or trauma specialist can offer a safe space where you can explore your pain without fear of judgment. They're not there to "fix" you, but to help you navigate the emotional roadblocks that trauma has left behind. Have you ever held back from talking about your trauma because you feared being misunderstood or judged? A professional can provide that non-judgmental, supportive environment that makes all the difference.

So, how do you go about finding the right therapist? It can feel overwhelming, especially when you're already dealing with the weight of your trauma. The first thing to keep in mind is that **therapy isn't one-size-fits-all**. Just like every person's trauma is different, every therapist has their own approach. The goal is to find someone who specializes in trauma and, more importantly, someone you feel comfortable with. Trust is crucial in the therapeutic process. It's okay to find someone who feels like the right fit. You deserve to work with someone who listens, understands, and creates a space where you feel safe to open up.

When you're searching for a therapist, there are a few things to consider:

- **Specialization**: Make sure the therapist has experience working with trauma. Trauma therapy is different from other forms of counseling because it often involves addressing deeply rooted emotional pain and developing specific coping strategies. Ask them about their background in trauma therapy—many therapists specialize in approaches like EMDR (Eye Movement Desensitization and Reprocessing), CBT (Cognitive Behavioral Therapy), or trauma-focused CBT, which are all effective for managing trauma.

- **Comfort Level**: You have to feel at ease with the person you're opening up to. After all, therapy is a partnership. Don't hesitate to have a consultation session before committing to a therapist. It's okay to ask yourself afterward, *Do I feel comfortable talking to this person? Do I trust them with my story?*

- **Therapeutic Approach**: Different therapists use different methods. Some might focus more on talk therapy, while others might incorporate mindfulness, bodywork, or even art therapy. Take the time to understand their approach. Does it resonate with you? Therapy should align with what makes you feel comfortable and supported.

And here's a tip: **don't be afraid to switch therapists if it's not working**. There's no shame in trying out different professionals until you find someone who clicks with you. It doesn't mean there's something wrong with you; it simply means that healing is personal, and you deserve to work with someone who truly helps you move forward. It's your journey, and finding the right guide is a big part of that.

Have you ever wondered what it would feel like to talk to someone who's been trained to listen without judgment? Someone who can not only hear your pain but offer tools to help you move through it? That's what therapy is about—working together with a professional to make sense of your trauma and find healthier ways to cope.

How do you know when it's time to seek help? It's different for everyone, but there are some signs that therapy might be the right next step for you. If you find that your trauma is interfering with your daily life—whether through anxiety, flashbacks, depression, or overwhelming emotions—it might be time to consider professional support. If you feel stuck, like no matter what you do, the trauma continues to weigh you down, therapy can provide a path forward. You don't have to wait until things are unbearable to reach out. In fact, seeking help early can make all the difference in how you heal.

And remember, **therapy is a tool—not a cure-all**. It's not about going to a few sessions and magically feeling better. It's about building a foundation, step by step, that helps you manage your emotions and reclaim your life. Sometimes, it's about learning to sit with the pain without letting it define you. Other times, it's about finding new perspectives that allow you to grow from your experiences. Healing from trauma takes time, but having the right professional alongside you makes it a little less daunting.

Practical Tips for Starting Therapy

1. **Start with a list of questions**: When you first meet a therapist, it's okay to ask them about their experience with trauma, what methods they use, and how they typically work with clients.
2. **Use online directories**: Websites like *Psychology Today* or *Therapy Route* allow you to filter therapists based on their specialties, location, and even insurance coverage.
3. **Give it time**: Building a relationship with a therapist doesn't happen overnight. It may take a few sessions before you feel fully comfortable opening up, and that's okay. Healing is a process.
4. **Consider group therapy**: Sometimes, hearing other people's stories and sharing your own in a group setting can be just as powerful as individual therapy. Group therapy provides a community of support where you can realize that you're not alone in your experiences.

So, where do you go from here? Think about what kind of support feels right for you. Do you need one-on-one sessions with a trauma specialist, or would group therapy provide a sense of connection? Whatever path you choose, just know that seeking professional help is an act of self-compassion, not weakness. It's saying to yourself that *I deserve healing and don't have to do it alone.*

End of Chapter Reflection

Trauma may leave scars, but it doesn't have to define your future. You've explored the different types of trauma, learned how grounding techniques can bring you back to the present moment, and discovered the healing power of sharing your story. Through these tools and insights, you've begun to see that trauma, while part of your journey, doesn't have to be the end of it. You're more than your pain, and healing is within your reach.

To deepen your understanding and start putting these practices into action, here's a 7-day challenge designed to guide you through the process of healing from trauma:

- **Day 1: Identifying Trauma**
  Spend time reflecting on the type of trauma you've experienced. Write down what memories or feelings come up and how they affect you. Acknowledge what you've been through without judgment.

- **Day 2: Grounding Through Senses**
  Practice grounding by focusing on your surroundings. Name five things you can see, hear, or touch. Use this technique whenever you feel overwhelmed, and note how it helps you stay present.

- **Day 3: Reclaiming Your Story**
  Write down a part of your trauma story. Focus on how you've survived it, not just the pain it caused. Reflect on the strength it took for you to make it through.

- **Day 4: Deep Breathing Practice**
  Spend five minutes practicing deep, controlled breathing. Notice how your body responds. Use this technique whenever your emotions feel too big to handle.

- **Day 5: Seeking Support**
  Reach out to someone you trust, whether it's a friend, family member, or therapist. Talk about your experiences, or simply share how you've been feeling lately. Reflect on how it felt to open up.

- **Day 6: Reflecting on Strength**
  Write down three ways in which you've shown strength, despite the trauma you've experienced. Reflect on how these strengths have helped you cope and move forward.

- **Day 7: Self-Compassion**
  End the week by practicing self-compassion. Write a letter to yourself, acknowledging your difficulties, but also offer forgiveness and kindness. Reflect on how this act of self-compassion feels.

As you move through this challenge, notice how these small steps bring you closer to healing. You may not erase the scars, but you can reclaim your sense of self and begin to rewrite your story.

Now, think about this: Have you ever looked in the mirror and felt like you didn't like what you saw? Trauma doesn't just affect how you feel—it can also impact the way you view your body. In the next part of our journey, we'll discuss the complex relationship between mental health and body image. How do your thoughts about your body shape your self-esteem? Together, we'll explore how you can begin to improve the way you see yourself, inside and out.

Chapter 8: Improving Body Image

"To be beautiful means to be yourself. You don't need to be accepted by others. You need to accept yourself." — Thich Nhat Hanh.

Body image is not about the reflection you see in the mirror; it's about the relationship you have with your body—*your thoughts, emotions, and beliefs* surrounding how you perceive your physical self. Every time you catch a glimpse of yourself or think about your appearance, those feelings are swirling around in your mind, shaping how you feel about yourself overall. For many people, this relationship can be complicated, even painful. Maybe you've felt the pressure to meet certain beauty standards or found yourself wishing your body looked different, thinking that if you just changed one thing, you'd feel better. But the reality is, when you focus too much on fitting into external ideals, it can take a toll on your mental well-being.

Think about the times you've compared yourself to others—whether it was a celebrity on social media, a friend, or even a stranger passing by. Those moments can leave you feeling inadequate, like your body is somehow "less than." It's a heavy weight to carry, especially in a society that constantly pushes images of what it thinks beauty should look like. Maybe you've felt frustrated, thinking, *"Why don't I look like that? What's wrong with me?"* The truth is, there's absolutely nothing wrong with you. The way you see your body is shaped by years of exposure to unrealistic standards, and that's where the struggle begins. It's like walking through a maze where every turn leads to a different message about what your body *should* be.

These struggles with body image can have a deep impact on your mental health. It's not just about feeling a little insecure—it can lead to constant self-criticism, anxiety, and even depression. Have you ever found yourself avoiding social situations because you didn't feel confident in how you looked? Maybe you skipped a beach day with friends because you didn't want to be seen in a swimsuit, or you turned down an invitation to an event because you didn't feel comfortable in your own skin. These feelings can isolate you, making you feel disconnected from the people around you and even from yourself. You might avoid looking at your reflection, thinking that ignoring it will make the discomfort disappear, but those negative feelings linger, affecting every aspect of your life.

But what if things could be different? What if you could change the way you see your body, not by altering your appearance, but by changing how you feel about it? Healing your relationship with your body isn't about achieving perfection or trying to fit into a certain mold. It's about learning to appreciate and accept your body for everything it is and everything it does for you. This shift in mindset is incredibly powerful, and while it doesn't happen overnight, it's one of the most freeing and transformative journeys you can take.

Start by asking yourself: *What would it feel like to truly accept my body, right now, exactly as it is?* Imagine being able to look at yourself with kindness instead of criticism. Instead of focusing on what you think is "wrong," you begin to appreciate what's right. Your body has carried you through every experience, every challenge, and every moment of joy and pain. It's resilient, and it deserves your love and respect.

Healing your relationship with your body begins with small, intentional actions. It's not about making a drastic change all at once—it's about taking one step at a time toward self-acceptance and body positivity. It's about challenging those negative thoughts that have been ingrained in your mind and replacing them with more compassionate ones. When you start to shift your perspective, you'll find that your confidence grows naturally, and the weight of unrealistic expectations begins to lift.

There's a sense of empowerment that comes with embracing who you are, just as you are. When you stop letting external standards dictate your worth, you reclaim your sense of self. You begin to see that beauty is not defined by how you look, but by how you feel in your own skin. The process of improving body image is deeply personal, but it's also incredibly rewarding. With each step you take, you move closer to a place of acceptance and peace.

Self-Acceptance Practices

One of the most significant steps in improving your body image is learning to cultivate self-acceptance. This means appreciating your body for what it can do, rather than focusing solely on how it looks. This change in perspective doesn't happen overnight—it takes time, patience, and daily practices that gently shift the way you see yourself. But, over time, these small efforts can build into a more positive relationship with your body, one grounded in kindness rather than criticism.

Think about how often you've looked in the mirror and immediately focused on what you didn't like. Maybe it's the shape of your nose, the curve of your hips, or the texture of your skin. It's easy to get caught in a self-criticism cycle, especially when surrounded by images of so-called "perfection." But self-acceptance invites you to take a step back from that negativity and look at yourself with fresh eyes.

Have you ever tried **mirror work**? It's a simple but powerful exercise that can change how you see yourself. The next time you stand in front of the mirror, instead of immediately zooming in on what you want to change, pause. Take a deep breath and focus on something you appreciate about your body. Maybe it's the way your eyes light up when you smile, or the strength in your legs that carries you through each day. It could even be something as small as the texture of your hair or the softness of your hands. The goal isn't to ignore the parts of your body you might not love yet—it's about balancing that critical voice with one that's kind.

At first, this exercise might feel a bit strange or uncomfortable. We're so used to picking ourselves apart that it can be hard to know how to be gentle with ourselves. But with practice, you'll notice a shift. Over time, the negative thoughts soften, and you begin to see yourself through a more compassionate lens. Each time you look in the mirror and choose to appreciate rather than criticize, you're sending a message to yourself: *I am worthy of love and respect, just as I am.*

Mirror work isn't the only way to practice self-acceptance. **Self-affirmation** is another powerful tool that can help reshape the way you think about your body. It involves repeating positive statements about yourself—especially about your body and your worth. If you've spent years telling yourself that you're not good enough or that you don't measure up, this might feel uncomfortable at first. But remember, just like any new habit, it takes time to settle in.

Try starting your day with a few affirmations like, "My body is strong and capable," or "I am deserving of love and kindness." Write these affirmations down on sticky notes and place them on your mirror, your desk, or anywhere you'll see them regularly. The more you repeat them, the more your mind begins to accept them as truth. At first, it might feel like you're just going through the motions, but over time, these positive words will begin to replace the critical voice in your head. Have you ever noticed how words have power? The things you say to yourself, even silently, shape the way you see yourself.

Let's imagine a scenario: You're getting ready for a big event, maybe a party or an important meeting. As you stand in front of the mirror, that familiar voice creeps in—*"I wish I looked different. I wish I was thinner, taller, prettier..."* Instead of letting those thoughts take over, what if you paused and said something kind to yourself instead? *"I'm grateful for the strength my body gives me,"* or *"I'm enough exactly as I am."* These small shifts in self-talk don't erase the challenges of body image, but they do create space for compassion.

Affirmations, much like mirror work, help to rewire the way you think about yourself. Have you ever noticed how easy it is to believe the negative things you say to yourself, even if they're not true? By consciously replacing those negative thoughts with positive affirmations, you're gradually teaching your mind to be kinder. It's like planting seeds—at first, it might feel like nothing is changing. But with time and repetition, those seeds grow, and you start to see the difference in how you treat yourself.

Another way to practice self-acceptance is through **gratitude for what your body can do**. Instead of focusing solely on appearance, shift your attention to your body's abilities. Maybe your legs carried you through a long walk, or your arms lifted a heavy grocery bag. Perhaps your body helped you through a tough day at work or allowed you to laugh with friends. When you appreciate what your body does for you, it becomes easier to show it kindness, even if it doesn't look exactly the way you wish it did.

Think about the times your body has supported you, even in small ways. Has it helped you play a sport, take care of your loved ones, or simply keep you moving through your day? When you start focusing on what your body does, rather than what it looks like, you build a deeper appreciation for it. You realize that your body is not just an image—it's your partner in life, carrying you through all your experiences.

Every step you take toward self-acceptance is a victory. It's a process, and some days will feel easier than others. But each time you practice mirror work, say an affirmation, or show gratitude for your body's abilities, you're building a stronger, healthier relationship with yourself. Over time, these practices become habits, and you'll find that the way you see yourself—and your body—begins to change.

Media Literacy

Every day, you're bombarded with images from all directions—social media, TV, magazines, and advertisements—all pushing a narrow, often unattainable definition of beauty. These platforms constantly present a version of "perfection" that makes you question your own body. Have you ever scrolled through Instagram or flipped through a magazine and felt that sinking feeling, thinking, *"Why don't I look like that?"* It's as though the world is telling you there's a standard you need to meet, but here's the truth: those images? They're not real.

What you see on your screen has likely been carefully curated, filtered, and even edited. Think about it—how often have you seen a celebrity or influencer post a flawless photo and later learned it was photoshopped or filtered to perfection? These images create a false narrative of what beauty should look like, and it's easy to get caught up in comparing yourself to something that doesn't even exist in real life. But what if you stopped and questioned these images instead of letting them define how you see yourself?

When you encounter an image that makes you feel inadequate, take a moment to pause. Ask yourself: *Is this image real? Has it been digitally altered or edited to fit a certain ideal?* Often, the answer is yes. Most of the images you see in the media are designed to sell you something—whether it's a product, a lifestyle, or an idea of beauty that makes you feel like you're not enough. But why let those messages define how you see yourself? Have you ever wondered how freeing it would be to let go of those comparisons?

Learning to critically analyze media messages is one of the most empowering things you can do. The next time you see an image that makes you feel "less than," ask yourself: *What is this image really trying to tell me?* Does it promote unrealistic standards that no one can truly live up to? Start breaking down these messages and recognize them for what they are—marketing tactics that play on your insecurities. Once you begin seeing through the illusion, you can regain control over how you view yourself.

The truth is, beauty isn't something that can be measured by a set standard or captured in a perfectly posed photo. It's not about fitting into someone else's idea of what you should look like. Real beauty comes from embracing your uniqueness, the qualities that make you, *you*. Think about it—have you ever admired someone not because of how they look but because of their confidence or how comfortable they are in their own skin? That's the kind of beauty that resonates with people, and it has nothing to do with filters or flawless skin.

Media literacy helps you take back your power. The more you question what you see, the more you begin to realize that those images you once idolized are, in fact, just illusions. So, the next time you find yourself comparing your body to someone's highlight reel on social media, remind yourself that you're only seeing a carefully crafted snapshot of their life. What would happen if you chose to celebrate your uniqueness instead of chasing an impossible standard? What if, instead of trying to fit into a mold, you focused on being the most authentic version of yourself?

Taking control of how you interpret media messages can also change the way you consume media. You don't have to follow accounts or consume content that makes you feel bad about yourself. Have you ever considered curating your feed to include more body-positive, diverse representations of beauty? Surround yourself with images that make you feel empowered, not diminished. This small action can make a big difference in how you see yourself each day.

Ultimately, media literacy is about reclaiming your right to define beauty on your own terms. It's about realizing that beauty isn't something the media can dictate to you—it's something you create within yourself. When you learn to see through the filters and edits, you realize that you're more than enough just as you are. Why should anyone else's definition of beauty take that away from you?

By becoming media-literate, you're not just challenging the messages you see—you're rewriting the narrative. You're choosing to see your value beyond what the media tells you is beautiful. And every time you do, you take one step closer to fully embracing your own unique, authentic beauty.

Body-Positive Lifestyle Changes

Improving your body image isn't about following the latest diet trend or forcing your body to fit into a specific mold. It's about making lifestyle changes that help you reconnect with your body in joyful, freeing, and supportive ways that support your overall well-being. These changes shift the focus from appearance to how you *feel* in your own skin, helping you cultivate a healthier, more positive relationship with your body.

Intuitive eating is one powerful approach that encourages you to listen to your body's natural signals—hunger, fullness, and satisfaction—rather than following rigid diets or food rules. Imagine what it would feel like to let go of the constant battle with food and simply honor your body's needs. When was the last time you ate without guilt, simply enjoying the experience? Intuitive eating invites you to tune into your body and ask yourself questions like, *"Am I hungry right now, or am I eating because I'm stressed or bored?"* By recognizing these cues, you can start to build a healthier relationship with food, one that's based on trust and care rather than restriction and shame.

It's not about labeling foods as "good" or "bad"—it's about balance and understanding how different foods make you feel. Have you ever noticed how your energy levels shift depending on what you eat? Paying attention to how certain foods impact your body helps you make nourishing and satisfying choices, not just for your physical health but for your mental and emotional well-being too. Intuitive eating encourages you to enjoy food as something that fuels your body and gives you pleasure, rather than as something to fear or control.

Another practice that helps improve body image is **joyful movement**. Instead of exercising with the goal of changing how your body looks, why not focus on moving in ways that feel good to you? The joy of movement comes from discovering activities that make you feel energized, strong, and connected to your body. It could be as simple as a walk in the park, dancing around your living room, or swimming at the beach. Movement doesn't have to be about burning calories or sculpting a particular physique—it's about celebrating what your body can *do*.

When was the last time you moved your body just because it felt good, not because you were chasing a specific fitness goal? Joyful movement is all about finding activities that bring you happiness and leave you feeling more alive. Whether it's yoga, cycling, or a fun dance class, the key is to focus on the enjoyment of moving rather than seeing exercise as a punishment or a means to an end. Exercise can become an act of gratitude for your body, a way of saying, *"Thank you for carrying me through this life."*

Even something as simple as **fashion choices** can influence how you feel about your body. Have you ever noticed how wearing clothes that make you feel comfortable and expressive can completely shift your mood? The clothes you choose to wear can impact your confidence and the way you carry yourself throughout the day. The key is dressing for *yourself*, not for someone else's expectations of how you should look. Fashion is a form of self-expression—whether you prefer bold colors, flowing fabrics, or cozy layers, what matters is how it makes you *feel*.

When you wear something that reflects your personality and makes you feel comfortable in your own skin, it shows. You stand taller, smile more, and exude a sense of self-assurance. Dressing for your body, rather than trying to fit into trends that don't align with who you are, empowers you to embrace your uniqueness.

What would happen if you chose to dress in a way that celebrated who you are, rather than trying to conform to someone else's idea of beauty? How much more confident would you feel if you allowed your clothes to reflect *you*—not a version of you that someone else wants to see?

These body-positive lifestyle changes—intuitive eating, joyful movement, and fashion choices—are about aligning with what feels right for *you*. They're about shifting the narrative from one of judgment and comparison to one of self-compassion and self-expression. When you stop trying to force your body into unrealistic standards and start honoring it for what it is, you open the door to a deeper, more loving relationship with yourself.

Now, take a moment to think: How often have you focused on changing your body instead of embracing it? What if, instead of battling against your body, you chose to celebrate it? What if the real beauty isn't about fitting into someone else's standard, but about living in harmony with the body you have, right now? Could it be that by simply making these shifts, you'll find a newfound sense of freedom and confidence?

End of Chapter Reflection

Body image is deeply personal, and it shapes how you see yourself in ways that can either uplift or weigh you down. Throughout this chapter, you've explored how your perception of your body impacts your mental health. You've seen how negative body image can lead to feelings of anxiety, depression, and isolation. But you've also begun to understand that there are ways to shift this perspective through self-acceptance, critical thinking, and lifestyle changes.

The journey to improving body image is not about perfection—it's about learning to embrace your body, as it is, with compassion and care. You've started to see how practices like mirror work, self-affirmation, intuitive eating, and joyful movement can reshape how you relate to your body. Every step you take toward self-acceptance brings you closer to feeling at peace with who you are.

To help deepen these insights and put what you've learned into action, here are a series of **exercises** that will guide you through strengthening your relationship with your body. Each exercise is designed to bring you closer to self-acceptance, encouraging you to engage with your body in new, compassionate ways:

- **Exercise 1: Mirror Affirmation Practice**
  Start your day by standing in front of a mirror. Instead of focusing on what you don't like, find at least one thing that you appreciate about your body. It might be your eyes, your hands, or even your smile. Say it out loud and give yourself permission to celebrate that part of yourself. As you repeat this daily, notice how it feels to speak kindly to your reflection. Does the discomfort begin to fade? Do you start to see your body in a new light?

- **Exercise 2: Media Awareness and Detox**
  For the next few days, become aware of how media is shaping your thoughts about body image. Scroll through your social media feed or watch an advertisement—what messages are being sent about beauty and body standards? Are they realistic? Take a moment to reflect on how these messages make you feel about yourself. Then, consciously reduce your media exposure. Unfollow accounts that promote unhealthy ideals, and replace them with ones that embrace diversity and body positivity. How does curating your media influence your self-esteem?

- **Exercise 3: Daily Positive Affirmations**
  Choose three affirmations that resonate with you—statements like, "I am worthy just as I am," or "My body deserves kindness and care." Write them down and place them somewhere visible, like your bathroom mirror or desk. Repeat these affirmations throughout your day, especially when negative thoughts arise. Over time, notice

how these words start to soften the critical voice inside and reinforce a more compassionate narrative about yourself.

- **Exercise 4: Intuitive Eating Check-In**
  Today, as you sit down to eat, take a moment to check in with your body. Are you eating because you're genuinely hungry, or are you eating out of stress or boredom? As you eat, pay attention to the textures and flavors, noticing how your body responds to the food. This isn't about restriction or dieting—it's about being mindful and reconnecting with your body's needs. How does this shift in awareness change your relationship with food and your body?

- **Exercise 5: Joyful Movement Exploration**
  Explore movement that brings you joy rather than focusing on burning calories or achieving a certain look. Whether it's dancing in your living room, taking a peaceful walk outside, or practicing yoga, engage with your body in a way that feels good. As you move, pay attention to how your body feels—are you more energized, relaxed, or connected? Reflect on how movement can become a source of self-expression and self-care, rather than a punishment or obligation.

- **Exercise 6: Fashion as Self-Expression**
  Tomorrow, choose an outfit that makes you feel comfortable and confident—something that allows you to express your unique personality. As you go through your day, notice how wearing clothes that feel good affects your mood and how you carry yourself. Does dressing for yourself, instead of meeting external expectations, bring a sense of freedom? Reflect on how style can be a tool for self-love and empowerment.

- **Exercise 7: Evening Self-Reflection**
  Before bed, take a few minutes to reflect on your progress in improving your body image. Write down one thing you've done today to be kind to yourself or your body. Maybe you noticed your posture during the day or allowed yourself to enjoy a meal without judgment. As you build these small moments of self-care, you're reinforcing a more positive relationship with your body. How does it feel to end the day with gratitude for yourself?

As you work through these exercises, pay attention to how they shift your perception of your body and your self-worth. Are you starting to see your body in a more compassionate light? What new realizations have surfaced as you've engaged with these practices? Remember, it's a journey—and each small step you take brings you closer to a more positive, loving relationship with yourself.

Now, let me ask you—have you ever wondered what it would feel like to have a clear plan in place to protect and nurture your mental health, not just when things get tough, but every single day? It's one thing to tackle challenges as they come, but what if you could be proactive, setting yourself up for long-term well-being? That's exactly what we'll discuss next. Together, we'll explore how to create your very own Personal Mental Health Plan—a guide that helps you navigate those hard moments while also building emotional resilience.

PART 3:
INTEGRATING STRATEGIES INTO DAILY LIFE!

Chapter 9: Creating a Personal Mental Health Plan

"A good plan today is better than a perfect plan tomorrow." — *George S. Patton.*

Taking charge of your mental health means having a clear roadmap that guides you through both the highs and the lows. A certain peace comes with knowing you have a plan in place—a strategy that helps you navigate tough moments while ensuring you continue to thrive when things are going well. A personal mental health plan is not just about managing the difficult times, but also about building a foundation that supports your emotional well-being in the long run.

Setting Clear Goals

The first step in creating a mental health plan is setting clear, actionable goals. You may have heard of SMART goals before—those that are Specific, Measurable, Achievable, Relevant, and Time-bound. These types of goals give you structure and focus, helping you stay on track as you work toward improving your mental health. Let's break down each component of the SMART framework and look at how you can apply it to your personal mental health goals:

- **Specific**
  A goal is most effective when it's specific. This means being clear about what exactly you want to achieve. Vague goals like "I want to feel better" or "I want to reduce my anxiety" are harder to measure and accomplish because they don't give you a concrete direction. Instead, think

about the details of what you want to accomplish. What actions will you take, and how will you know when you've achieved it?

For example, instead of saying, "I want to manage my stress," a more specific goal would be, "I will practice deep breathing exercises every morning to manage my stress levels." This clearly defines the action you're going to take (deep breathing), when you'll do it (every morning), and what outcome you're working toward (managing stress). Making your goal specific gives yourself a clear starting point and a defined path forward.

- **Measurable**

  A measurable goal allows you to track your progress. This is important because it gives you tangible evidence of how far you've come and helps you stay motivated along the way. Ask yourself: How will you know when you've made progress? What indicators will show that you're moving toward your goal?

  Let's take the previous example of practicing deep breathing every morning. You could make this goal measurable by adding, "I will practice deep breathing for 10 minutes each morning." Now you have a concrete way to measure your progress—you can track how many days you've completed the practice and how long you've done it. You could even keep a journal to note how you feel before and after each session. By making your goal measurable, you can look back and see the changes happening, which can be incredibly motivating.

- **Achievable**

  Your goal should be realistic and attainable. Setting goals that are too big or unrealistic can lead to frustration and burnout, especially when it comes to mental health. Think about your current circumstances and what's actually doable for you. Ask yourself: Is this goal something I can reasonably accomplish given my resources and time?

For example, if you're struggling with severe anxiety, it might not be realistic to say, "I will eliminate all anxious thoughts within a week." Instead, an achievable goal could be, "I will reduce my anxious thoughts by practicing mindfulness for 10 minutes every day for the next two weeks." This goal is both realistic and attainable because it focuses on consistent small actions rather than expecting an immediate, dramatic change. It's important to set goals that challenge you, but also make sure they're within reach so that you can build confidence as you achieve them.

- **Relevant**
A goal is relevant when it aligns with your broader mental health needs and priorities. It should matter to you and contribute to your overall well-being. Ask yourself: How does this goal fit into my bigger picture? Does it address the specific mental health challenges I'm facing?
For instance, if one of your main challenges is managing stress at work, a relevant goal could be, "I will take a 5-minute break every hour during my workday to practice mindfulness." This goal directly addresses your stress management and is aligned with what you need right now. Relevance ensures that you're focusing on goals that will have a meaningful impact on your mental health, rather than pursuing goals that might not be as beneficial for your specific situation.

- **Time-bound**
A time-bound goal gives you a deadline or timeframe, which adds a sense of urgency and helps you stay accountable. Without a timeframe, it's easy to procrastinate or lose focus. Ask yourself: When do I want to achieve this goal by? What is my timeline for taking action?
Using the earlier example of deep breathing, you could make this goal time-bound by saying, *"I will practice deep breathing for 10 minutes each morning for the next 30 days."*

Now you have a clear timeline that helps you stay committed to the goal. As you approach the end of those 30 days, you can evaluate your progress, see how far you've come, and decide if you want to continue or adjust your goal. Having a timeframe gives your goal structure and helps you stay on track.

Example of a SMART Goal
Now, let's put it all together with a specific example: "I will practice mindfulness meditation for 10 minutes every day for the next 30 days to help manage my stress levels."

- **Specific**: Mindfulness meditation is the specific practice.
- **Measurable**: The goal is to do it for 10 minutes each day.
- **Achievable**: 10 minutes of meditation is realistic and fits into your daily routine.
- **Relevant**: The goal is tied to managing stress, which is a priority for your mental health.
- **Time-bound**: The goal has a clear timeframe of 30 days.

As you create your own SMART goals, think about what areas of your mental health you want to focus on—whether it's reducing anxiety, improving sleep, or building resilience. Break your goals down into actionable steps, and use the SMART framework to ensure that each goal is clear, measurable, and achievable. By doing this, you're setting yourself up for success and taking meaningful steps toward improving your well-being.

Developing a Routine

Once you've set your goals, it's time to incorporate them into your daily life. Developing a routine that supports your mental health is crucial for turning those goals into reality. Think about a day that feels scattered—where you're constantly jumping from task to task, and by the time the day's over, you realize you haven't taken a moment to breathe or check in with yourself. A routine can help prevent those chaotic days by providing structure and stability, offering you intentional moments to prioritize your well-being.

The key to creating a routine is to focus on self-care practices that resonate with you. What activities make you feel more balanced or bring a sense of calm? For some, it might be something as simple as listening to music or taking a few minutes to read a book that brings them joy. Others might find that engaging their senses—whether through cooking, gardening, or working with their hands—helps them unwind and refocus. The beauty of routines is that they're personal, and you get to decide what works best for you.

For instance, if you enjoy spending time outside, you might incorporate a quick walk into your routine. Even 10 minutes of fresh air can refresh your mind and lift your spirits. Imagine taking that time to clear your thoughts or notice the beauty of your surroundings—a gentle breeze, birds chirping, or the sun on your face. It's a simple practice, but one that can help you feel grounded and present. If walking isn't your thing, maybe you carve out time to sit quietly in a cozy space and enjoy your favorite drink, allowing yourself a moment to just be.

Another idea might be to build **creativity** into your routine. Have you ever tried starting your day with a creative task, like doodling, writing, or playing an instrument? Even if it's just for a few minutes, doing something creative first thing in the morning can set a positive tone for your day. Creativity doesn't have to mean being an artist—it can be as simple as cooking a new recipe or rearranging your workspace in a way that inspires you. The key is finding what energizes and excites you to take on the day.

When building your routine, it's important to start small. You don't need to make sweeping changes all at once. Have you ever noticed how overwhelming it can feel when you try to change too many things at once? It's easy to lose motivation. Instead, begin with one or two small habits. If your goal is to unwind after a long day, you might start by setting aside 10 minutes in the evening to relax with a cup of herbal tea or read a few pages of a book. Over time, these small moments can become part of your routine, offering a sense of comfort and consistency.

It's also crucial to keep your routine flexible. Life is unpredictable, and there will be days when things don't go according to plan. Maybe you don't have time for your usual morning ritual or your evening relaxation gets interrupted—that's okay. Routines aren't meant to be rigid; they're meant to support you. The key is to return to your routine when you can, without feeling guilty or discouraged if you miss a day. Your mental health plan is about progress, not perfection.

Another element to consider in your routine is **social connection**. Maybe you set aside a few minutes each week to check in with a friend or loved one. This could be as simple as sending a text or scheduling a quick phone call. These small interactions remind you that you're not alone and provide a mental health boost through connection. Sometimes, talking to someone about your day can bring a sense of relief and help put things into perspective.

As you shape your routine, think about the small but meaningful actions that make you feel supported and calm. Whether it's stepping outside for a few minutes, getting creative, or sharing a laugh with a friend, the routine you build should reflect what brings you balance. Remember, it's not about getting it perfect—what matters is that you're taking the time to care for yourself in ways that feel natural and achievable.

Adjusting Your Plan

Of course, a mental health plan isn't something you create once and then never look at again. Just like your life shifts and changes, so do your mental health needs. That's why it's essential to check in with yourself regularly and make adjustments as needed. Think about it—what worked for you a few months ago might not feel as effective now. Maybe your routine has started to feel a little stale, or perhaps a new challenge has surfaced that requires more of your attention. Whatever the case, giving yourself the freedom to adapt and make changes is important.

Your mental health plan is like a living document—it grows and evolves with you. Have you ever tried sticking to a plan that just doesn't feel right anymore? It can be frustrating when you're forcing yourself to do something that no longer aligns with where you are mentally or emotionally. And that's okay! Sometimes we outgrow the strategies that once worked for us, and the best thing we can do is shift gears.

Let's say you've been practicing a specific self-care routine for a while, but it's started to feel more like a chore than something that brings you peace. Maybe at one point, going for a morning walk was your go-to way to clear your mind, but lately, it just feels exhausting. Instead of pushing through, give yourself permission to switch things up. Maybe now you'd prefer a slower start to your day, like enjoying a quiet moment with your favorite book or spending time journaling instead. The key is to listen to what your mind and body need in this moment, not what worked for you in the past.

It's also important to consider that life can throw unexpected curveballs your way. You might find yourself dealing with a new stressor—perhaps a demanding project at work, family responsibilities, or a sudden life change. When that happens, your mental health plan should be flexible enough to accommodate these shifts. It's not about throwing your whole plan out the window, but rather adjusting it to better fit your current reality. Maybe that means setting more manageable goals or focusing on stress-relief techniques that help you cope with the extra pressure.

Have you ever noticed how sometimes a slight adjustment can make all the difference? Maybe you're feeling overwhelmed, and simply scaling back on certain tasks can ease that pressure. Or perhaps introducing something new, like a fun hobby or a creative outlet, can breathe fresh life into your routine. The most important thing to remember is that your mental health plan isn't set in stone—it's meant to change as you do.

Think of it as a dynamic toolkit that you can customize as your needs evolve. If one tool stops working, swap it out for another. For example, if mindfulness used to help you manage stress but now feels repetitive, maybe it's time to explore other options like guided imagery or spending more time in nature. You might even find that your goals change altogether. What felt like a priority a few months ago might not hold the same weight today, and that's perfectly fine. Your mental health journey is personal and is all about what works best for you right now.

So, how do you know when it's time to adjust your plan? One way is to check in with yourself regularly. Every few weeks, ask yourself: How am I feeling? Is my current routine supporting my mental health, or do I feel like I'm just going through the motions? Is there anything new in my life that's affecting my well-being? These reflections can guide you in fine-tuning your plan to better meet your needs.

Remember, flexibility is your friend. Life changes, and so do you, so don't hesitate to make adjustments when necessary. It's not about perfection—it's about staying responsive to your mental health and giving yourself the tools to thrive, even when things get messy.

End of Chapter Reflection

Creating a *Personal Mental Health Plan* is not just about setting goals—it's about taking an active role in your well-being and building a roadmap that guides you through life's ups and downs. Throughout this chapter, you've explored how to set clear goals, build supportive routines, and track your progress to ensure that you're staying on the right path. But most importantly, you've seen that your mental health plan is something that can grow and evolve with you as your needs change.

Think about how you can begin to integrate these ideas into your daily life. What steps can you take today to set clear goals for your mental health? How might developing a routine help you stay grounded, even during stressful times? Each action you take brings you closer to feeling more balanced and in control of your mental well-being.

To help you put this into practice, here are several **exercises** that will guide you through building and refining your mental health plan. Each exercise is designed to help you stay proactive and engaged in your mental health journey:

- **Exercise 1: Goal-Setting Session**
  Set aside 15 minutes today to write down your top three mental health goals. Be specific and use the SMART goal framework. Once you've written them down, break each goal into smaller, actionable steps. Reflect on how achieving these goals will positively impact your daily life.

- **Exercise 2: Morning Routine Design**
  Take some time to think about what your ideal morning routine looks like. What practices or activities help you start your day with a sense of calm and purpose? Create a simple routine that you can follow each day. Start small—

maybe it's five minutes of meditation, stretching, or journaling—and build from there.

- **Exercise 3: Mood Tracking Journal**
  For the next week, keep a daily journal where you record your mood at different points throughout the day. Pay attention to any patterns—what activities make you feel better, and what situations cause stress? Use this journal to gain insight into your emotional health and refine your mental health plan accordingly.

- **Exercise 4: Self-Check-In**
  Every few weeks, schedule a personal check-in where you review your mental health plan. Are your goals still relevant? Is your routine supporting your mental well-being? Take this time to adjust any parts of your plan that no longer serve you and consider introducing new practices that resonate with you.

- **Exercise 5: Positive Habit Building**
  Choose one habit that you'd like to introduce into your daily routine that supports your mental health—whether it's practicing gratitude, mindful breathing, or regular exercise. Set a goal to practice this habit for the next 30 days and reflect on how it improves your mood and mindset.

Now that you've laid the groundwork for your mental health plan, it's time to consider another crucial aspect of well-being: *building a solid support system.* Have you thought about the role that others play in your mental health journey? Who do you turn to when life gets tough? Together, we'll explore how to cultivate a network of people who uplift, support, and inspire you. After all, mental health isn't something you have to manage alone—having the right people by your side can make all the difference.

Chapter 10: Building a Support System

"Surround yourself with only people who are going to lift you higher."
— *Oprah Winfrey.*

How often do you take a moment to consider the relationships that surround you? The people in your life play a significant role in shaping your mental well-being, whether you realize it or not. Your support system is like a lifeline—on days when you feel like you're treading water, these are the people who help keep you afloat. Having a strong network of social support is essential for maintaining mental health because it gives you a sense of belonging, security, and connection. When you feel supported, you're more likely to face challenges head-on, knowing you're not doing it alone.

But it's not just about having people around; it's about having the *right* people. Relationships can be a double-edged sword. Have you ever found that certain people seem to drain your energy, while others uplift you? That's because not everyone in your life will offer the kind of support you truly need. It's important to surround yourself with those who genuinely care about your well-being—people who are willing to listen, understand, and offer encouragement without judgment. These are the relationships that nurture your mental health, providing the foundation for emotional resilience.

The role of a supportive network goes beyond just being there during crises. True social support is about having people in your life who celebrate your victories, no matter how small, and help you find strength in moments of doubt. It's about the friend who listens when you need to vent, the family member who checks in on you during tough times, or the colleague who notices when you're not quite yourself and offers a kind word. These individuals make it easier to cope with life's stressors because they remind you that you're not navigating this journey alone.

You may already know the value of a good support system, but sometimes it's hard to take a step back and assess your current relationships. Have you ever noticed how being around certain people leaves you feeling drained or anxious, even if nothing particularly negative happens? Those are signs that some relationships may not be serving your mental health. On the other hand, some leave you feeling understood and empowered—those are the connections worth nurturing.

Identifying Supportive People

So, how do you identify the people who are truly supportive? It all starts with a deep reflection on the relationships in your life. Think about the people who make you feel safe, understood, and valued. These are the individuals who listen without judgment, the ones who offer empathy rather than solutions when you're struggling. Who do you naturally turn to when you're feeling overwhelmed or seeking advice? Take a moment to consider those who have consistently been there for you—not just during the high points in your life, but also during the times when you've felt lost or vulnerable. These people will often stand by you, no matter what life throws your way.

Supportive people come in many forms. It might be a close friend who has seen you through various stages of your life, a family member who offers you unconditional love, or even someone in your community—a neighbor or coworker—who has always been a reliable presence. What's important is not how long you've known them, but how they make you feel. Do you feel comfortable being your true self around them? Do you feel heard and validated, even when you're sharing difficult or uncomfortable feelings? Those are the people worth holding close.

However, identifying support doesn't always mean sticking to the people you've known the longest. Sometimes, the most supportive connections are the ones that come into your life unexpectedly. Have you ever met someone who, despite not knowing you for years, seems to naturally understand you? New connections can often offer a fresh perspective and much-needed emotional support, especially when they approach your struggles with an open mind and heart. Don't underestimate the power of these newer relationships. Even a brief but genuine connection can provide you with the encouragement and care you need, especially during challenging times.

There's also an important distinction to be made between quality and quantity when it comes to building a support system. It can be tempting to think that having a large network of people around you means you're well-supported, but that's not always the case. Sometimes, having too many surface-level relationships can leave you feeling lonelier than ever. Have you ever found yourself surrounded by people, but still feeling disconnected? That's because not all connections are meaningful. You might have a large circle of acquaintances, but if those relationships don't offer the depth and care you need, they can leave you feeling unfulfilled.

In contrast, one or two reliable people can have a far greater impact on your mental health than a large group of casual friends. These individuals check in on you not just when it's convenient but when they sense you might need them the most. They remember the small details about your life, offer their time and attention without expecting anything in return, and provide a safe space where you can express your thoughts and emotions without fear of being judged or dismissed. With these people, you don't have to wear a mask or pretend that everything is okay when it's not. You can simply be yourself.

It's also important to recognize that supportive relationships aren't one-sided. Healthy connections require reciprocity. Are you able to be there for these people when they need support? Do they allow you to give as well as receive? Relationships where both parties can lean on each other when needed are the ones that strengthen over time. Being surrounded by individuals who only take without giving can leave you feeling depleted rather than supported.

When evaluating your support system, take note of how you feel after interacting with certain people. Do they leave you feeling uplifted and cared for, or do you feel drained and anxious? Trust your instincts—your emotional response to these interactions is a powerful indicator of whether or not someone is truly supportive. It's important to be mindful of this, as some relationships may need reevaluating if they consistently leave you feeling worse than before.

Building and maintaining a support system is an ongoing process. It's not about keeping every person you've ever known close to you—it's about being intentional with your connections, seeking out people who offer genuine support, and allowing those relationships to evolve naturally. Strengthening your support system means nurturing the relationships that matter most while being open to new connections that bring positive energy into your life. Ultimately, it's about surrounding yourself with people who not only understand you but also inspire you to be the best version of yourself.

Joining Support Groups

While individual relationships are crucial, sometimes connecting with a broader community can offer additional layers of support. Have you ever considered joining a support group? Whether online or in-person, support groups bring together individuals who are facing similar challenges. There's something incredibly powerful about being in a space where people truly understand what you're going through, even if you've never met them before. It's a sense of shared experience that can be hard to find elsewhere.

Support groups provide a unique opportunity to share your story, express your feelings, and listen to others who are experiencing similar struggles. Imagine being part of a group where someone talks about the same anxious thoughts you've been wrestling with, or the overwhelming sense of isolation that depression can bring. Hearing someone else put your feelings into words can be validating, reassuring you that you're not the only one dealing with these emotions. And just as importantly, these groups are spaces free of judgment. Everyone is there for the same reason: to offer and receive support in a compassionate, understanding environment.

For example, if you're dealing with anxiety, joining an anxiety-focused support group could introduce you to new coping strategies that others have found helpful, such as breathing exercises, journaling, or grounding techniques. Or if you're struggling with depression, hearing others share their journeys might encourage you to try something new, like establishing a simple daily routine or practicing mindfulness. These groups often provide practical tools and emotional support to incorporate into your mental health journey.

There are many types of support groups available. For example, organizations like the National Alliance on Mental Illness (NAMI) offer peer-led groups that cover a wide range of topics, from anxiety and depression to bipolar disorder and grief. If you prefer the flexibility of an online setting, platforms like *7 Cups of Tea* or *Reddit's Mental Health Support Community* allow you to connect with others from the comfort of your own home. In-person groups can also offer a more personal connection, allowing you to build relationships over time with people in your local community.

If you're unsure where to start, many mental health organizations offer directories for both local and online support groups. The idea of joining a group might feel daunting at first—after all, opening up about your personal struggles to a group of strangers can seem intimidating. But consider this: everyone in the group has felt that same nervousness at some point. Taking that step to join a community of supportive individuals can be one of the most impactful decisions you make for your mental health. You'll not only find comfort in knowing you're not alone, but you'll also gain valuable insights from people who truly understand what you're going through.

End of Chapter Reflection

Your support system is one of the most vital tools in maintaining your mental health. The people who surround you—whether friends, family, or community members—play an integral role in your emotional well-being. Through this chapter, you've explored the importance of social support, how to identify the right people to lean on, and how effective communication strengthens these connections. You've also seen how joining support groups can expand your network and provide additional comfort during challenging times.

Building and maintaining a support system takes effort, but the rewards are immeasurable. As you strengthen these connections, you'll find that they offer you stability, encouragement, and a sense of belonging. Remember, you don't have to navigate life's challenges alone—there are people ready to walk alongside you.

To help reinforce what you've learned, here's a 7-day challenge designed to help you build or strengthen your support system. Each day, you'll focus on an aspect of connection, communication, or self-reflection to ensure that you're nurturing the relationships that matter most.

- **Day 1: Reflect on Your Current Support System**
  Take some time to reflect on the people in your life who offer genuine support. Who do you feel comfortable turning to when you need help? Write down their names and how they make you feel.

- **Day 2: Strengthen One Key Relationship**
  Reach out to one person from your list and check in with them. This could be a friend, family member, or coworker. Let them know you appreciate their support and share how you've been feeling lately.

- **Day 3: Communicate Your Needs**
  Think about one area of your life where you could use more support. Practice communicating this need to someone in your support system. Be clear about what kind of help you're asking for.

- **Day 4: Set a Healthy Boundary**
  Identify one relationship where you feel your boundaries could be stronger. Practice expressing a respectful boundary to protect your emotional well-being.

- **Day 5: Explore a Support Group**
  Research a support group that aligns with your mental health journey. Whether it's online or in-person, take a step toward learning more about how a group could benefit you.

- **Day 6: Practice Active Listening**
  Strengthen your relationships by being fully present with someone when they share something with you. Offer your full attention and show empathy in the conversation.

- **Day 7: Reflect on Your Progress**
  Look back on the steps you've taken this week. How has focusing on your support system impacted your sense of connection and well-being? What changes have you noticed in how you relate to others?

As you continue to grow in your relationships, remember that connection is a two-way street. How you show up for others also influences how they show up for you. Nurturing these bonds creates a foundation of support that can carry you through life's ups and downs.

Now, have you ever wondered why, even in moments of stillness, your mind keeps racing? Or why you sometimes feel disconnected from the present, caught in a loop of past worries or future anxieties? That's where mindfulness and meditation come in. These practices help ground you, bringing you back to the present moment with clarity and calm. In the next section, we'll explore how mindfulness and meditation can be powerful tools to quiet the noise and restore balance to your mental state.

Chapter 11: The Power of Mindfulness and Meditation

"Quiet the mind, and the soul will speak." — Ma Jaya Sati Bhagavati.

What if you could quiet the constant chatter in your mind, even if just for a few moments each day? Imagine how that might transform your ability to manage stress, reduce anxiety, and stay grounded. This is where mindfulness and meditation come in. They offer you a way to calm your mind, be fully present in your life, and connect with a deeper sense of peace. In a world full of distractions, these practices allow you to slow down and focus on what really matters—your mental and emotional well-being.

Mindfulness is about being fully aware of the present moment, without judgment. It's not about clearing your mind of thoughts but about observing those thoughts with curiosity, letting them come and go without getting caught up in them. When you're mindful, you allow yourself to truly experience what's happening right now, rather than worrying about the future or replaying the past. This simple act of paying attention can work wonders for your mental health. It brings a sense of clarity and calm that is often missing in our busy lives.

But why is mindfulness so beneficial for your mental well-being? Research has shown that practicing mindfulness can reduce symptoms of anxiety and depression, improve focus, and even help with emotional regulation. When you're mindful, you're more in tune with your thoughts and emotions, which means you can respond to challenges with greater awareness and less reactivity. It allows you to pause before reacting, creating space for healthier responses to stress and difficult situations.

Daily Mindfulness Practices

Incorporating mindfulness into your daily life doesn't require hours of meditation or solitude. It's about finding small moments to be present, even during the most mundane activities. For instance, have you ever tried mindful eating? Instead of rushing through your meal, take the time to notice the flavors, textures, and aromas. How does the food taste? What sensations do you feel as you chew? This practice helps you connect more deeply with the experience of eating and encourages a greater sense of gratitude for the nourishment you're giving your body.

Another simple practice is mindful walking. When was the last time you took a walk without your phone or any distractions? As you walk, focus on the sensation of your feet touching the ground, the rhythm of your breath, and the movement of your body. Notice the environment around you—the colors, the sounds, the smells. Mindful walking brings your awareness back to the present moment, giving your mind a much-needed break from the constant flow of thoughts.

Mindfulness can be woven into even the most routine parts of your day. You might practice mindfulness while washing the dishes, taking a shower, or brushing your teeth. The goal is to be fully present in whatever you're doing, paying attention to each moment with a sense of openness and curiosity. Over time, these small moments of mindfulness add up, creating a more centered and peaceful way of living.

Beginner Meditation Techniques

If you're new to meditation, you might wonder where to begin. The thought of sitting still with your thoughts can feel intimidating, but meditation doesn't have to be complicated. A great way to start is with guided meditation. There are plenty of apps and online resources that offer short, easy-to-follow meditations, guiding you through the process of calming your mind and focusing your attention. Simply find a quiet place, sit comfortably, and allow yourself to be led through the meditation.

Breathing exercises are another excellent entry point into meditation. Have you ever noticed how your breath changes when you're anxious or stressed? Deep, intentional breathing can calm your nervous system and bring a sense of immediate relief. Try taking slow, deep breaths, counting to four as you inhale, holding for a moment, and then exhaling for another count of four. This simple practice can help center your mind and body, bringing you back to the present moment.

Mantra meditation is another option for beginners. In this practice, you focus on a positive word or phrase and repeat it softly to yourself during the meditation. Words like "peace" or "calm" can serve as anchors, gently guiding your mind back whenever it starts to wander. Repeating a mantra can help you stay focused and deepen your meditation practice, creating a sense of inner peace.

Advanced Mindfulness Strategies

For those who are more experienced with mindfulness and meditation, you might want to explore deeper techniques that further enhance your practice. Body scans are an excellent way to connect with your physical self and bring attention to areas of tension or discomfort. During a body scan, you mentally "scan" each part of your body, noticing how it feels without trying to change anything. It's a great way to cultivate awareness and relaxation.

Loving-kindness meditation is another powerful practice that involves directing compassion toward yourself and others. In this meditation, you silently repeat phrases like, "May I be happy. May I be healthy. May I be at peace," extending these wishes first to yourself and then to others, including loved ones and even people you may struggle with. This practice nurtures empathy and compassion, helping you build more meaningful connections with yourself and others.

Visualization is another advanced technique where you imagine a peaceful place or a positive outcome, allowing your mind to focus on something soothing or uplifting. It's a way to use your mind's natural creativity to bring a sense of calm and positivity into your life, especially during times of stress.

For those looking to deepen their meditation practice further, organizations such as the *Thich Nhat Hanh Foundation, Transcendental Meditation (TM) Organization,* and *Self-Realization Fellowship* offer teachings and resources to guide you on your journey. These communities provide not only techniques but also a sense of shared experience, helping you feel connected to a larger world of mindfulness practitioners.

End of Chapter Reflection

Mindfulness and meditation offer you the chance to step out of the chaos and reconnect with yourself. Throughout this chapter, you've explored the power of being present, learning how mindfulness can bring clarity and peace to your life. You've discovered simple ways to incorporate mindfulness into daily routines, practiced beginner meditation techniques, and learned about more advanced methods for deepening your practice. The main takeaway? These practices are accessible to anyone and can profoundly impact your mental and emotional well-being.

To help you integrate these concepts into your daily life, here's a 7-day challenge designed to guide you through mindfulness and meditation practices. Each day, you'll focus on one aspect of mindfulness, gradually building a routine that can bring lasting peace and clarity.

- **Day 1: Mindful Eating**
  During one meal today, focus entirely on the act of eating. Pay attention to the flavors, textures, and smells of your food. Notice how it feels to eat mindfully without distractions.

- **Day 2: Deep Breathing Exercise**
  Take five minutes to practice deep breathing. Inhale for a count of four, hold for four, and exhale for four. Notice how your body feels before and after.

- **Day 3: Mindful Walking**
  Take a walk outside, leaving your phone behind. Pay attention to your steps, the feel of the ground beneath your feet, and the environment around you.

- **Day 4: Mantra Meditation**
  Choose a positive word like "calm" or "peace" and repeat it softly to yourself during a five-minute meditation. Focus on the word whenever your mind starts to wander.

- **Day 5: Body Scan Meditation**
  Spend ten minutes practicing a body scan. Start from the top of your head and move slowly down to your feet, noticing any sensations in each part of your body.

- **Day 6: Loving-Kindness Meditation**
  Practice loving-kindness meditation by silently repeating kind phrases to yourself: "May I be happy. May I be healthy. May I be at peace." Extend these wishes to others as well.

- **Day 7: Quiet Reflection**
  Set aside ten minutes for quiet reflection or meditation. Let your mind rest and observe your thoughts without judgment. Notice how this practice affects your mood and energy.

As you continue exploring mindfulness and meditation, think about the moments when you feel the most disconnected from yourself. What if you had the tools to stay grounded, even in the most challenging times? Maintaining mental health is not just about self-care when things are going well—it's about resilience during difficult moments. Let's explore how you can protect your mental well-being, even in the toughest situations.

PART 4:
SUSTAINING YOUR JOY

Chapter 12: Maintaining Mental Health in Challenging Times

"Resilience is accepting your new reality, even if it's less good than the one you had before." — Elizabeth Edwards.

Life has a way of throwing unexpected challenges at us. Whether it's a major life event, a setback in your personal or professional life, or the emotional toll of navigating a tough situation, maintaining your mental health during these moments can feel overwhelming. Yet, it's in these difficult times that building resilience becomes crucial. Resilience is not about avoiding struggles but learning how to adapt and thrive despite them. It's about bouncing back, even when the circumstances seem less than ideal.

Resilience Building

Building resilience is like strengthening a muscle—it takes time, practice, and the right techniques. One of the most effective ways to develop resilience is by learning how to manage stress. When life gets difficult, stress can often spiral out of control, making challenges seem even bigger than they are. Have you noticed how your mind races or how your body feels tense during stressful moments? Techniques like deep breathing, mindfulness, and time management can help you regain control. Taking small breaks, setting boundaries, and learning to say "no" when necessary can also create space for you to recharge.

Adaptability is another key aspect of resilience. The truth is, life rarely goes according to plan. Things change—sometimes unexpectedly. Being adaptable means being able to shift your mindset and approach when things don't go as you envisioned. Rather than resisting change, embracing it with flexibility allows you to find new solutions and perspectives. Have you ever found yourself stuck, not because of the situation itself, but because you were holding on to the way you *wanted* things to be? Letting go of rigid expectations can be liberating, and it opens the door for growth, even in hard times.

Emotional regulation is equally important. It's natural to feel overwhelmed when things don't go as planned, but how you respond emotionally can either help or hinder your ability to navigate difficult times. Practicing self-compassion, recognizing when you need to take a step back, and allowing yourself to feel your emotions without being consumed by them are all part of building resilience. You don't have to have it all figured out—sometimes, simply acknowledging that you're doing your best is enough.

Coping with Setbacks

Setbacks are an inevitable part of life, but they don't have to derail your progress. Have you ever experienced a moment when it felt like all your efforts were undone because of one misstep? It's easy to feel defeated when things don't go as expected, but setbacks are not the end of the road—they are opportunities for growth. One way to handle setbacks is by having a crisis plan in place. This doesn't mean expecting the worst, but rather having strategies ready for tough times. Whether it's a trusted person to call, a calming routine, or a list of resources that help you refocus, having a plan can prevent you from feeling overwhelmed.

Relapse prevention strategies are also helpful, particularly if you've been on a mental health journey for a while. If you've made progress in managing anxiety, depression, or other mental health challenges, there may be times when old patterns resurface. And that's okay. Relapses happen, but they don't erase the progress you've made. Learning to recognize early signs of a relapse—

whether it's feeling more anxious, losing motivation, or withdrawing from others—can help you address the situation before it spirals. The key is not to judge yourself but to take small steps toward getting back on track.

Developing a Positive Mindset

It can feel impossible to stay optimistic when you're facing setbacks or challenges, but maintaining a positive mindset can make all the difference. This doesn't mean ignoring difficulties or pretending everything is fine when it's not. Instead, it's about focusing on what *can* be done and recognizing that every problem has a solution, even if it's not immediately clear. Have you ever found yourself dwelling on the worst-case scenario, only to realize later that things weren't as bad as you imagined? Shifting your mindset from "What if it all goes wrong?" to "What if I find a way through this?" is a small but powerful shift that keeps you moving forward.

One way to cultivate positivity is through gratitude. By focusing on the things that are going well, even when life feels challenging, you begin to train your mind to see the silver linings. Maybe you've had a difficult week, but did a friend reach out with support? Did you manage to complete a task, even if it felt small? Acknowledging these victories, no matter how minor, can uplift your spirit and remind you that progress is still happening, even in tough times.

Lifelong Learning for Mental Health

Mental health is not a one-time goal to achieve; it's a lifelong journey. Just as you continue to learn new things in other areas of life, constantly improving your mental well-being is essential for long-term health. Have you ever noticed how, when you stop challenging yourself, you begin to feel stagnant? Continuous learning, whether through reading, taking courses, or trying new mental health practices, helps you stay mentally agile. Each new skill you develop becomes another tool in your toolkit for maintaining mental health, especially in challenging times.

Consider setting aside time for regular mental health check-ins or exploring new techniques that help you manage stress. Whether it's exploring mindfulness practices, learning about emotional intelligence, or diving into new ways of thinking, each piece of knowledge you acquire enhances your ability to maintain mental health over the long term.

Setting New Goals

As you continue your journey, it's important to set new mental health goals reflecting your current needs and growth. Have you ever felt like you've plateaued or lost direction? Setting goals gives you something to aim for and motivates you to keep moving forward. Whether it's creating a better work-life balance, improving your self-care routine, or tackling a specific challenge like managing anxiety, new goals help keep your mental health journey dynamic.

The key to successful goal-setting is breaking your goals down into manageable steps. Instead of trying to accomplish everything at once, focus on small, achievable tasks that lead to a larger objective. Each step forward, no matter how small, brings you closer to your goal, reinforcing a sense of progress and accomplishment.

Celebrating Successes
It's easy to focus on the next challenge or goal, but taking a moment to celebrate your successes is just as important. Have you ever downplayed an achievement because it didn't feel big enough? But every victory, no matter how small, deserves recognition. Whether it's finishing a task you've been avoiding, handling a difficult conversation with grace, or simply getting through a tough day, these are all reasons to celebrate. By

acknowledging your successes, you build momentum and reinforce the belief that you can handle whatever comes your way.

Celebrating successes doesn't have to be extravagant. It could be as simple as taking a moment to reflect on how far you've come or rewarding yourself with something that brings you joy. These small celebrations boost your motivation and remind you that progress is happening, even if it doesn't always feel like it.

End of Chapter Reflection

Maintaining mental health during challenging times requires resilience, adaptability, and a positive mindset. As you've explored, building resilience through stress management, emotional regulation, and adaptability creates a strong foundation for navigating difficulties. You've also learned how to cope with setbacks without losing progress, how to develop a positive mindset to stay motivated, and why lifelong learning and setting new goals are essential for sustaining mental well-being.

Now it's time to put these ideas into practice. To help guide you, here's a 7-day challenge designed to reinforce what you've learned:

- **Day 1: Reflect on Resilience**
  Write down three situations where you showed resilience in the past. How did you manage to push through? Reflect on the strengths you used during those times.

- **Day 2: Crisis Planning**
  Create a simple plan for how you'll handle future setbacks. Identify one person you can reach out to for support and one activity that helps you manage stress.

- **Day 3: Gratitude Practice**
  Start the day by writing down three things you're grateful

for, focusing on the positives, even in challenging times. Reflect on how this shifts your mindset throughout the day.

- **Day 4: Positive Affirmations**
  Choose three affirmations that resonate with you. Repeat them throughout the day, especially when facing difficult moments. Notice any changes in your self-talk.

- **Day 5: Learn Something New**
  Set aside 20 minutes to read or learn something new related to mental health. It could be an article, a podcast, or a new technique. Reflect on how this new knowledge can help you in your journey.

- **Day 6: Set a New Goal**
  Write down one mental health goal for the next week. Break it down into small steps and focus on one task to move toward that goal today.

- **Day 7: Celebrate Your Successes**
  Take time to reflect on your week. What small victories have you achieved? Celebrate them by treating yourself to something you enjoy, whether it's a quiet moment, a favorite meal, or simply acknowledging your progress.

As you continue to build resilience and maintain your mental health, think about how these small practices have impacted your life. How have you grown? What new strengths have you discovered in yourself?

Conclusion

A BIG Congratulations! Seriously, take a moment to let that sink in. You've come so far, and it's not easy to prioritize your mental health in the way you've done. This is a huge accomplishment, and it's worth celebrating. Think about it—you've just made it through some of the toughest topics out there: *anxiety, depression, trauma, self-esteem, and body image*. And now, look at you. You've got a toolkit full of strategies and techniques to help you reclaim your joy and truly take control of your well-being.

Remember when we first talked about managing anxiety? You now know how to ground yourself when things start to spiral. You've learned to build routines that can lift you when you're feeling low, and you've discovered the power of positive affirmations to shift your mindset when those negative thoughts start creeping in. You've tackled self-esteem with kindness, boosting your confidence through small, meaningful steps. You've even begun the healing process for past traumas, using visualization, self-forgiveness, and other methods that help you move forward. And don't forget—you've started to appreciate your body for all it is, and that's no small thing. That's huge.

But here's the thing: none of this is just for the tough times. These tools? They're meant to be *lived*—every single day. Maybe you'll start your mornings with a moment of calm, or end your evenings by reflecting on something you're grateful for. Maybe you'll pause throughout the day to remind yourself of the progress you're making, even if it feels small. These little practices can make a big difference, and they're now part of who you are. Life will keep throwing challenges your way—no doubt about that—but now you're prepared to handle them with more grace, strength, and resilience.

Let's be real for a second—this journey is far from over. Reclaiming your joy isn't a one-time thing; it's a process. There will be setbacks, and that's totally okay. What matters is that you keep going, even when things feel tough. Growth takes time. Healing takes time. And you? You've got the patience and the determination to see it through. Each little step forward builds on the last, even if it doesn't always feel like progress in the moment.

Now, let's talk about how to make these strategies part of your life—because that's where the magic happens. These tools you've learned aren't just for when you're feeling down but for every day. It's about creating a routine that keeps you grounded, whether it's practicing those calming techniques when stress pops up or taking a moment to reflect on your emotions at the end of a long day. Maybe you'll even use affirmations to remind yourself that you are enough, that you are capable, that you're growing every day. The more you integrate these practices into your life, the more natural they'll feel, and the more you'll start to see real, lasting change.

But here's the truth: growth doesn't happen overnight. There will be days when you feel like you're not moving forward, when progress seems slow or nonexistent. And that's when it's most important to be patient with yourself. Look how far you've come already! You've made a commitment to yourself and your mental health, and that's no small thing. Every single day brings new chances to apply what you've learned, and each time you do, you reinforce the progress you've made.

You've laid the groundwork for something incredible. But this is just the beginning. As you continue on your journey, there will be challenges—and that's okay. Healing isn't a straight path, and it's totally normal to have moments where you feel stuck or frustrated. But the important thing is that you keep going. On the tough days, remind yourself of everything you've learned, and trust that you have what it takes to keep moving forward.

And don't forget—you're not alone. While your path is unique, there's a whole community of people, myself included, who believe in you and are cheering you on. Your journey matters. Your healing matters. And you deserve the joy, peace, and fulfillment you're working toward. Every act of self-care, every positive thought, every bit of progress proves that you can live a life that brings you happiness and contentment.

So, as you move forward from here, remember this: you are resilient. You are strong. And you are on a path that's leading you toward the life you deserve. Keep going—you've already come so far, and there's so much more ahead for you. You've got this!

Writing a Letter to Yourself

One of the most personal and impactful exercises you can do as you move forward is to write a letter to yourself. This isn't just any letter—it's a space for you to reflect on how far you've come, celebrate your growth, and set intentions for the future. It's a way to document your journey, offering yourself words of kindness and encouragement for the road ahead. Writing a letter to yourself allows you to see, in your own words, the progress you've made and the resilience you've built.

How to Write Your Letter:

1. **Reflect on Your Journey**: Start by acknowledging the journey you've taken throughout this book and your mental health journey as a whole. Reflect on the challenges you've faced, the strategies you've implemented, and the progress you've made. It doesn't matter how big or small the progress feels—each step is worth celebrating.

2. **Offer Kindness and Encouragement**: Write to yourself with the same compassion you would offer a dear friend. What words of encouragement do you need to hear?

Remind yourself of your worth, your resilience, and the strength you've shown. Acknowledge that it's okay to have tough days and that you have the tools to overcome them.

3. **Set Intentions for the Future**: As you look ahead, what hopes and goals do you have for your mental health journey? Write about the steps you want to take, the habits you want to build, and the mindset you want to cultivate. Be specific and optimistic—this is your chance to set intentions for continued growth.

4. **Revisit Your Letter**: Keep this letter in a safe place and revisit it whenever you need a reminder of your progress. During moments of doubt or difficulty, this letter will serve as a beacon of hope and a reflection of how far you've come.

Writing this letter is not just a reflective exercise—it's a gift to your future self. It's a reminder that no matter what challenges come your way, you have the strength, wisdom, and resilience to overcome them.

Help Others Heal: Your Feedback Can Make a Difference

If this book has touched you, I kindly ask that you consider sharing your experience by leaving a ***"positive feedback review"*** on Amazon. Your thoughts, your story, and your feedback mean the world to me, and they also have the power to make a difference in someone else's life. You see, when others read your review, they're not just learning about the book—they're hearing your personal journey. And that could be exactly what someone else needs to find the courage to start their own path toward healing. We all know how it feels to be searching for something that can truly help, and your review could be the key that leads someone else to find this book when they need it most.

"Thank you so much for taking the time to read this book. Your journey is truly special, and I'm deeply honored to have been a part of it. Remember, no matter how small, every step you take brings you closer to reclaiming the joy and peace you deserve. Keep going, trust in yourself, and know that you are never alone on this path. You have the strength within you to create a life filled with happiness and fulfillment."

Carol Moore

About the Author

Carol Moore has dedicated over 30 years to her work as a psychologist and psychotherapist, helping individuals navigate various mental health challenges. Her extensive experience has given her deep insight into the emotional struggles people encounter, regardless of their background or circumstances.

Throughout her career, Carol has been a source of compassionate guidance, providing practical tools to help her clients heal and thrive. She strongly believes in each person's ability to achieve personal transformation. Whether addressing self-doubt, managing depression and anxiety, or restoring confidence, Carol equips individuals with the tools they need to regain control of their lives and move forward with renewed purpose.

In addition to her one-on-one coaching, Carol is a passionate advocate for mental health awareness, regularly speaking at events and sharing her expertise through workshops and community programs. Her commitment to helping others extends beyond her practice, as she strives to break down the stigma surrounding mental health and empower individuals to seek the support they deserve.

Discover More from the Author!

If you found the strategies in this book helpful, I'm excited to introduce my previous book, **Reclaim Your Self-Esteem**. This guide takes an even deeper look into building confidence, self-worth, and emotional resilience, especially for those who have felt the sting of rejection. Rejection can leave deep scars, but this book is designed to help you rise above, offering practical tools and compassionate insights to help you rediscover your inner strength and embrace your true value.

Whether you've struggled with self-esteem issues for years or are just beginning to focus on self-acceptance, *Reclaim Your Self-Esteem* offers a clear and supportive roadmap to rebuild lasting confidence and create a more positive relationship with yourself.

Ready to take the next step on your journey toward self-love, resilience, and confidence? >Click here to get *Reclaim Your Self-Esteem* on Amazon Kindle!<

Recommended Reads for Your Journey

As you continue to explore your mental health and well-being, here are some highly recommended books that can offer further insights, inspiration, and tools for personal growth:

- **Reasons to Stay Alive** by Matt Haig
  A powerful and uplifting exploration of living with anxiety and depression, offering hope and encouragement.
- **You Are Here** by Thich Nhat Hanh
  A gentle and accessible guide to mindfulness and living fully in the present moment.
- **Peace Is Every Step** by Thich Nhat Hanh
  Discover how small, mindful actions can bring joy and peace into everyday life.
- **Laugh Again** by Charles Swindoll
  This book reminds us of the importance of joy and laughter, even during life's most challenging times.
- **The Book of Joy** by Dalai Lama & Desmond Tutu
  Two spiritual giants share their wisdom on finding lasting happiness, no matter your circumstances.
- **The Joy of Small Things** by Hannah Parkinson
  A heartwarming book that celebrates finding happiness in life's everyday, simple moments.
- **Daring Greatly** by Brené Brown
  Learn how embracing vulnerability can lead to courage, connection, and a deeper sense of self-worth.
- **Radical Acceptance** by Tara Brach
  A powerful guide on how to embrace ourselves and our lives with compassion, no matter the circumstances.
- **The Four Agreements** by Don Miguel Ruiz
  A simple yet profound framework for achieving personal freedom and peace of mind.

These books offer different perspectives on mental well-being, joy, and self-discovery, making them wonderful companions as you continue your journey toward healing and personal growth.

Printed in Great Britain
by Amazon